Presented To:

From:

D

D1019351

OTHER BOOKS BY SAM SILVERSTEIN

The Success Model

No More Excuses

Non-Negotiable

Making Accountable Decisions

The Lost Commandments

NO MATTER WHAT

THE 10 COMMITMENTS OF ACCOUNTABILITY

BY SAM SILVERSTEIN

© Copyright 2018—Sam Silverstein

All rights reserved. This book is protected by the copyright laws of the Unites States of America. This book may not be copied or reprinted for commercial gain or profit. The use of short quotations or occasional page copying for personal or group study is permitted and encouraged. Permission will be granted upon request. For permissions requests, write to the publisher, addressed "Attention: Permissions Coordinator," at the address below.

SOUND WISDOM
P.O. Box 310
Shippensburg, PA 17257-0310

For more information on publishing and distribution rights, call 717-530-2122 or e-mail info@soundwisdom.com.

Quantity Sales. Special discounts are available on quantity purchases by corporations, associations, and others. For details, contact the Sales Department at Sound Wisdom.

While efforts have been made to verify information contained in this publication, neither the author nor the publisher assumes any responsibility for errors, inaccuracies, or omissions.

While this publication is chock-full of useful, practical information, it is not intended to be legal or accounting advice. All readers are advised to seek competent lawyers and accountants to follow laws and regulations that may apply to specific situations.

The reader of this publication assumes responsibility for the use of the information. The author and publisher assume no responsibility or liability whatsoever on the behalf of the reader of this publication.

ISBN 13 HC 978-1-64095-016-0
ISBN 13 eBook 978-1-64095-017-7
ISBN 13 TP: 978-1-64095-080-1

For Worldwide Distribution, Printed in the U.S.A.

Cover/jacket design by Geoff Silverstein
Interior design by Terry Clifton

Library of Congress Cataloging-in-Publication Data
Names: Silverstein, Sam, author.
Title: No matter what : the 10 commitments of accountability / by
    Sam Silverstein.
Description: Shippensburg, PA : Sound Wisdom, [2018] | Includes
    bibliographical references and index.
Identifiers: LCCN 2018000820| ISBN 9781640950160 (alk. paper) | ISBN
    9781640950177 (ebook)
Subjects: LCSH: Responsibility.
Classification: LCC BJ1451 .S547 2018 | DDC 170--dc23
LC record available at https://lccn.loc.gov/2018000820

1 2 3 4 5 6 7 8 / 21 20 19 18

DEDICATION

This book is dedicated to the potential in all people that is discovered either by embracing the Ten Commitments of Accountability in their life and becoming an Accountable Leader or because they are fortunate enough to have an Accountable Leader in their life.

ACKNOWLEDGMENTS

Many people have played a part in creating this book. Without their help it would be impossible to complete a project of this magnitude.

Thank you to my wife, Renee, my daughter and outstanding editor Sara Ferrara, and Sharon Miner.

Thank you to my editors at Sound Wisdom; you really made a huge difference in this project. Thank you also to the entire Sound Wisdom team. You are amazing to work with and my secret weapon!

CONTENTS

PREFACE

By Sam Silverstein

Accountability is the toughest subject I have ever studied. I have been doing this for 25 years and every day I discover a new depth and a new understanding of accountability. I was ten years into studying the basis for individual and organizational improvement before I even identified that accountability was the foundation. It was another ten years before I was able to move past the side of accountability that is filled with statements like "I am going to hold them accountable," "I need my people to be more accountable," and "I wish people would just do what they say they are going to do!" All of these statements connect to the physical. They connect to doing. They connect to using accountability as a whip to get people to work harder, do more, and produce more money for someone.

Accountability is not a physical subject. The purpose of this book is to explore the spirit of people and the spirit of an organization as it is defined by the Accountable Leader™.

Accountability is not a way of doing.
Accountability is a way of thinking.

This single statement alone opens the locker to the depth of what accountability really can be in the life of a person and of an organization. When we stop focusing on doing and turn our attention to what we are thinking, then real transformation occurs: we grow beyond the way we currently think, and a different outcome is produced in our life and our organizations.

Accountability is not about the tasks, reports, job descriptions, and deadlines. Accountability is about how you think about people.

The real power in accountability is revealed in the connections between people—the relationships that flourish—when commitments are made and kept. You will never be accountable to someone if you do not have a relationship with them. The most accountable people I see are masters of building relationships. The most accountable organizations we work with have created a culture where relationships are strong.

The dictionary defines *accountability* as "an obligation or willingness to accept responsibility or to account for one's actions."[1] Simplified, accountability is keeping your commitments to people! You are not accountable to things. You are accountable to people.

Accountability is a choice. It is a choice that each and every person must make for themselves. You cannot force someone to be accountable. You cannot demand that people are accountable and get a positive result.

As individuals we have to make an active decision that we want to live an accountable life. We have to decide that we want the rich relationships that both produce accountability and flow from living a life of accountability. This desire is encoded into our character. Our character is either one by design, where we have taken the time to think about what we believe and value, what those values mean to us, what the foundation for our values is, and how our values show up in our daily life. Or, we have a character by default, and we do none of that.

Accountability is keeping your commitments to people.

---

1 "Accountability," The Merriam-Webster Online Dictionary, accessed November 3, 2017, http://www.merriam-webster.com/dictionary/accountability.

In an organization, we can create a place where people want to be accountable. We do that through the organizational culture. Like with an individual's character, an organization's culture is either one by default, in which anything goes, or one by design. When an organizational culture is one by design, it has been defined by the organizational values.

This journey has transformed my life, and it can transform your life too! When I started to think differently about accountability, I started to make different decisions—I started to act differently, and I began to get different results. I see people differently, and I see myself differently. My view on what is possible for the people around me has expanded greatly. And guess what? My view on what is possible for me in my life has exploded with potential. I did not see it coming, but I know that if you embrace the ten commitments that I share in this book, you will discover the same, or greater, possibilities in your life and in the lives of people around you also!

Meaningful transformation does not happen because we change what we do. This is a common trap into which people and companies fall. They do not like the results they are getting so they say, "It is time to do things differently." Or, they say, "I have to start changing how I do things." We frequently see this around the first of the year. People make New Year's resolutions. The diet and fitness industries are dependent on this. Diet book sales zoom and fitness club memberships skyrocket in January.

The reason we eventually change back to our old way of being or doing is because we tried to change our actions without addressing the underlying way of thinking that is necessary to achieve the real transformation we desire. When we change how we think, then we will change what we do. Only then can we achieve real, lasting transformation.

The clients that we work with who want to be better but fail in the process are always the ones that are focused on changing behavior. They try to mandate different procedures, and they demand certain actions. On the other hand, the clients who are highly successful in the transformation they seek are always the ones who embrace the reality that it is what they are thinking that is either holding them back or moving them forward. They look to adjust, change, and expand how they think so that they can grow and improve.

Yes, it means saying, "How I am thinking is not right or is not serving us to the best possible effort." And saying that what you are doing is not working is easier than admitting that what you believe and think is wrong.

Accountability is the highest form of leadership.™ When it comes to leadership, we traditionally focus on all the wrong things. It's time to change that. Great communication skills will not make you a great leader, and not having great communication skills will not keep you from being a great leader. Charisma does not make you a great leader. History is filled with charismatic people who championed evil, hatred, and negative causes.

Accountability is the highest form of leadership.™

You don't have to have a certain personality to be a leader. It does not matter if you are gregarious or if you are soft-spoken. Leadership is an understanding. It is a way of thinking, not a way of doing. When you think a certain way, something happens. That something is a direct flow from what a leader is thinking. What leaders think about is the people they lead, their community, and what is right and wrong.

Leadership is not about developing your personal skills, telling better stories, dressing a certain way, or saying common leadership catch phrases. Leadership is always and forevermore about the people you lead. It is about developing your people, not yourself. And while there is nothing wrong with growing as a person, great leaders focus on taking what they learn and using it to help their people grow.

Leaders are always thinking about their people.

This is where accountability comes in, because accountability is about the commitments between people. The Accountable Leader makes ten very specific commitments to the people they lead. This not only applies to leadership in a company, but it applies to leadership in one's family and community as well.

Accountability is always going to be about your heart, not your head. We learn in school how to do. Every course that I took in college was connected to how to do something. I took courses on how to do marketing, how to do management, how to do accounting, how to do finance, and how to do customer service.

But accountability is about what is in your heart. This is a significant deviation from all the business tactics that are taught. But guess what? Everyone knows all of those tactics, and they can take you and your company only so far. What is in your heart is unique to you, and that is what you connect to people through. It is through your heart that you will build an army of people who will stand by your side on the darkest of days to ensure you are successful.

The 10 Commitments of Accountability come from the leader. They go from leadership to the people they lead and then back from the people they lead to leadership. It is not the other way around. Leadership cannot "go in there" and demand that this happens from their employees without them doing it first.

The only time you become a leader is when you are accountable. You become accountable when you are committed.

There are 10 Commitments of Accountability.

1. Commitment to the truth
2. Commitment to what we value
3. Commitment to "It's all of us"
4. Commitment to stand with you when all hell breaks loose
5. Commitment to the faults and failures as well as the opportunities and successes
6. Commitment to sound financial principles
7. Commitment to helping individuals achieve their potential and be their best
8. Commitment to a safe place to work
9. Commitment to your word is your bond
10. Commitment to a good reputation

This is at the core of what leadership is. If the leader is doing it, then everyone will do it!

Leadership is the power and ability to lead people. Leadership is beyond the physical. It is a power. It is a spiritual thing. Leadership is directly connected to valuing people, building relationships with people, committing to people, and always putting the people you lead before yourself.

Just because someone holds a position does not make that person a leader. Just because you are the CEO of a company does not mean that you are accountable, or that you tell the truth, or that you have sound financial principles, or that your word is your bond. It is not the position that tells us that. It is only when you walk the walk that your accountability becomes evident. And you can walk the walk without a title or position.

When you acknowledge that leadership is a responsibility and that you are first and foremost responsible for the people you lead, you are on your way to becoming an Accountable Leader. When you commit to your people and put them first, they know it and they will respond in a powerful way. They win, and guess what? You win too.

The 10 Commitments of Accountability are all about this journey of valuing people and committing to them, *No Matter What*!

Introduction

WHAT IS A COMMITMENT?

I am good with ideas. We all have strengths, and creating ideas is mine. I come up with ideas for my friends to utilize both personally and professionally, I formulate ideas that my clients can use in their organizations, and I create ideas that apply to my business. Over the years, I have formulated a lot of great ideas that have made a significant difference for the people around me and for myself.

When I look at the decisions I regret most in my personal or my professional life, I realize that I do not regret any decisions to try something new. What I regret is that I did not stick with some of those ideas. I regret not being committed to those ideas to the point of seeing them through to success. I honestly believe that I have given up on many ideas that, if I had been sincerely committed to them, could and should have led to significant success. It does sadden me to think of some of the opportunities I have missed out on because of a lack of commitment.

Today I am very careful about which creative ideas I take on. Just because something is a good idea does not mean that it is right for me. I know this and find that if I am selective in what I take on, my time and energy is focused, I am committed, and more often than not I achieve success. Having experienced the lack of positive outcomes that result from not being committed has taught me to be choosy in what I commit to and, when I do commit, to go all in and make it happen.

A Commitment Unleashes Power and Potential

There is a power that comes with commitment. What is that power? Power is a force you cannot see. It always produces results, and it is 100 percent guaranteed. The power of commitment will not fail you. Whatever you are committed to will produce a result for you. The fact that you are committed creates positive results. That is the power.

The power of commitment is transformational. It can transform us, the people around us, our organizations, and even our world.

Commitment unleashes potential. It allows you to become your best. One of the greatest transformations that commitment produces is the development of your character.

A COMMITMENT INVOLVES CHALLENGES AND SACRIFICES

Commitments are not easy. Your accountability will often be tested by challenges and conflicts: Are you going to keep your commitment even in the face of personal loss, in the midst of a crisis, or when it is not in your best interest to do so? A commitment has to do with character. Everyone is committed when it is easy, but when a conflict shows up so does the truth about whether or not you are committed. This is where your accountability is manifested. This is where your character is developed.

Just as a plant has to push through the earth to see the sun and grow, we too have to "push through" our challenges and conflicts and keep our commitments. It is in those moments that we grow as people. That blade of grass you see outside is pushing up through earth that is much heavier than itself. It is not easy. The plant goes through enormous stress to surface from the ground. Pushing through is not easy for plants, and it is not easy for us. Yes, we will have stress. Yes, we will have to work hard. And yes, we will be able to persevere and make it. In that moment that we overcome a difficulty to keep a commitment, we become something else—something better and something that will never go back.

Not only are commitments not easy; life is not easy. Anyone who achieves greatness and significance has made tremendous sacrifices. A sacrifice is serious. A sacrifice is not giving something up that is extra or unnecessary. It is giving up something important in order to do or achieve something that is of even greater significance.

We do not always see those sacrifices. We just see success on television or in the news and forget what went into it. That sacrifice always came because of some sort of commitment. The athlete committed to spending hours each day for years to develop his skill set. The doctor committed to spending hours each day for years learning about medicine. The entrepreneur with seemingly "overnight success" committed to spending years learning her trade and building a business in anonymity before achieving the success that we get to see.

A Commitment Is No Matter What

When we define accountability as "keeping one's commitments to people," it is easy to look past the word *commitment*. It is easy to think, "Oh yeah, I know what a commitment is. Everyone knows what a commitment is. It is when you say 'yes,' or 'I will,' or maybe even 'I do.'"

The reality is that people view commitments differently. Commitment is an incredibly powerful word. Without defining what a commitment is, we would undermine the definition of accountability.

A commitment is "No Matter What." Just because you hit tough times does not mean you need to move on or that it is time to quit. Just because something is hard does not mean you should do something else. Where is the commitment in that?

A commitment is a pledge. It is a promise. It is not a maybe, or a hopefully, or a probably. It is an absolute. It is a No Matter What.

A commitment is "No Matter What."

There is a seriousness in making a commitment. There is another level of commitment where it gets into your DNA, where you do not even think about the possibility of not doing it. This is the level of "No Matter What." This is the level that a true leader and accountable person reaches.

This definition of commitment will totally change the way you see everything. No Matter What™ has become my personal mantra. When you see everything through this lens, conviction takes on an entirely new meaning. What is possible expands because you are not going to give up along the way. Relationships are deepened because the people around you know that you have their back, always and every time. That is because it is a No Matter What!

When you take the position of No Matter What, you are not looking to hedge. You are all in. You will never be looking for a way out. You will only seek a way in. When you take the position of No Matter What, you develop a reputation for being reliable. Everyone around you knows where you stand in any situation. They know they can depend on you regardless of circumstances, and this frees them to focus on moving forward. When they know they can depend on you, you will discover that you can also depend on them. It becomes mutual.

There is a power that comes with a commitment.

In any situation and in any relationship, there are only three possible positions to take: *no, maybe,* and *yes. No* is obvious. *Maybe* means it is possible, but it also means it might not be possible or will not happen.

When our children were younger, they would ask my wife, Renee, if they could do something or if we could go somewhere. Sometimes the answer would be "yes" and sometimes the answer would be "no." Many times the answer was "maybe." "Maybe" meant the door was open but that it was not guaranteed. Actually, "maybe" was usually code for "I do not want to say 'no' so I am saying 'maybe,' but 'most likely' the answer will end up being 'no,' though it is still possible." Whew! Over time, when the kids heard Renee say, "Maybe," they came to learn what it meant and would respond, "Oh, that means 'no.'"

The real problem is when someone says, "Yes," but it really is a "maybe." This is not a commitment. This is someone who is not reliable. And over time people come to know that a "yes" from that person does not mean "yes." Because the person is not reliable, his or her credibility suffers. They lose the personal power that comes from a reputation of No Matter What.

Are you looking for a way out or are you looking for a way in?

Yes is a commitment, and a commitment is No Matter What. When you take this position, you will move heaven and earth to make it happen. This means your commitments make you a far more powerful individual, not only in the eyes of the people around you, but also in your actual ability to make something happen.

When people know you are committed to them, the power of a commitment grows even stronger. The people to whom you commit know that you believe in them, that you trust them, that you want them to succeed, and that you meet their needs before your own. This is the way an accountable person and a great leader operates.

Leaders are guarded with what they say. They think before they speak. When they do speak, what they say is based on what they believe and value. They do not just spout off randomly. They know what they are saying. A leader always remembers what they say. Part of commitment is being careful to remember what you say and agree to. Not remembering that you promised to do something is not an acceptable excuse for not doing it.

People who live No Matter What are guarded by what they say and are not "moved by the moment." They make their decisions and promises based on what they really believe, feel, and can deliver on.

A Commitment Requires Honesty and Transparency

Honesty and transparency are the core of keeping your commitments. In a work environment people do not easily commit to people they do not know and trust. Leaders get to know the people they lead and allow those people to get to know them in return. When leaders are transparent, you have the opportunity to get to know them. Do the people in your organization or in your life know you? Do they really know you?

Your belief in a cause or mission may be enough for you to sacrifice for people you are working to support or whose lives you are helping to improve. You give from your heart, and you want to make a difference. It does not matter that you do not know the specific people. You know the cause. You know the challenges they face. You know the difference in their lives that you can make.

But in an organization, you may not sacrifice for someone you do not know. And it is only when you know someone that you can care for him or her. The real key is that leaders always care for their people first!

An important person in my organization is my assistant, Sharon. We have daily discussions on accountability both organizationally and personally. We study the subject, develop depth to our philosophies, work with clients to help leaders and their organizations, and write speeches. It has not always been smooth sailing. Early on, we did not really know how to communicate with each other. And by early on I am talking about for three-plus years. We were constantly at each other's throats. Sharon could not believe that I did not fire her, and I could not believe that she did not quit. It was that rough sometimes.

The thing is that we knew each other. We knew each other's families. We knew each other's values. We were both committed to building a more accountable world. Sharon was committed to me and my mission, and I was committed to her.

We worked through those tough years and have built a wonderful friendship and developed a powerful ability to work together as a result. I know that she would always be there for me, and I believe she feels the same way.

A COMMITMENT REQUIRES CONSISTENCY, CLARITY, AND EQUALITY

When you have a track record of No Matter What, there is a consistency. Your actions are always consistent with your words. It is that consistency of No Matter What that becomes a significant part of the underpinning of your character.

To have a commitment, there has to be clarity. You have to know what it is that you are really committing to. You have to know the impact and the importance of the commitment. It is moving when you commit to something meaningful and deliver on that commitment.

People commit because they want to be part of something positive. They want to be a part of something that is bigger than them. They have a desire to be better. They want to contribute to a relationship and the betterment of someone else.

Organizations have the ability to offer all of that through their values. Employees are expected to live out the values. Whatever the leader is willing to commit to the employees will commit to. It becomes a reciprocal commitment.

A commitment has to do with equality. It has to do with fairness. When you're talking about an accountable culture, it cannot be one-sided.

When we work with an organization, we always find that if people in that organization are not being accountable, the leader isn't being accountable in the first place. It always starts with that leader. We always look at what leadership might be doing or if there are challenges, flaws, or weaknesses in the leadership. The truth may hurt, but it is the truth. Once we find those things that can be improved upon within the leadership, leadership can make changes. If leadership will get better, their team will get better. Everything rises and falls on leadership.

Our best clients are those clients where the leader says, "I want to get better." And then they are consistent about sharing that knowledge with the people they lead. They are saying, "If I am better at the same time that my team is getting better, then we are getting better as an organization."

Like I said, if the leader commits, then everyone else is going to commit. Without commitment what do you have? You have uncertainty and instability. There is doubt and inconsistency. None of these things produce an environment in which people enjoy working or that fosters tremendous success.

Everything rises and falls on leadership.

Without commitment, people do not bond. Relationships are key to communication and success. The organizations with the best relationships will outperform their competition every time. People working together, helping each other, and having each other's backs creates a high-productivity environment. It also creates a place where people like to work, which leads to great customer service and exceptional performance. It will not be like this without a unilateral commitment to the company's values.

A COMMITMENT REQUIRES COURAGE

It takes courage to commit. People have a hard time with what is not known. When you make a commitment, you do not always know how it is going to play out. You do not know what obstacles will come up. You do not know what possible opportunities you may have to say "no" to in order to keep your commitment.

Commitments are not always safe.

People often worry about what they are going to have to give up when they commit.

A lot of people like to be safe, and commitment can be risky business. Ask people if they are doing their dream job, and most times the answer will be "no." This is because people tend to play it safe. Playing it safe is what holds people back. We are talking about risk, and people are usually risk averse. What they do not understand is that through the commitment they will receive far more than what they may give up.

Not committing is the easy way out. Not committing does not take fortitude. It does not take consistency. You do not have to pay a price in time, energy, or possible lost opportunity. You avoid the tough decisions when you do not commit. In taking the easy way out, you lose all opportunity for personal growth, development, and gain.

A COMMITMENT BRINGS FREEDOM AND OTHER POSITIVE QUALITIES

At the level of No Matter What there is freedom. You are a slave to nothing and no one. The power that flows through you at the level of No Matter What allows you total freedom to follow your beliefs and do what you know to be right.

Positive qualities are produced in our lives when we commit. Those qualities are trust, respect, loyalty, credibility, influence, and accountability. In addition, we are able to build more meaningful relationships. Even friendship and love are produced when you are willing to commit.

If you would not want any of these traits in your life or in the organization at which you work, speak now or forever hold your peace. Exactly! Trust, respect, loyalty, and the other high-performance qualities allow us to operate at a high level in our lives and in our organizations. And we see people and companies all the time that lack in these areas. They are the people with whom we do not want to hang out and the companies at which we do not enjoy working or which we will not recommend to our friends and family.

Commitment is not a way of doing. It is a way of thinking.

A commitment is something you give. My commitment to you is not based on whether you keep your commitment to me. That would make my commitment conditional. My commitment is No Matter What!

This is not a tactical subject. This is not a way of doing. This is a way of thinking. It is permanent. It is absolute. Most people are looking for options. They are looking for an easy-out clause—an "in case something comes up." People want wiggle room, but it can't be that way.

Accountability is not a way of doing. Accountability is a way of thinking. Commitment is not a way of doing. Commitment is a way of thinking. A way of thinking will always produce a result, and when it comes to accountability and commitment that result is incredibly positive and unbelievably powerful.

A Commitment Requires Passion

In order for people to be committed to something they need to be inspired and passionate. They have to have a reason to commit.

The inspiration comes from the leader. Everything flows from the head. Whatever the head is committed to is going to impact the direction that the organization goes. Whatever the leader is consistent and steady with is the direction in which the organization will go.

So, if the leader is wishy-washy, the organization will be wishy-washy. If the leader is focused, the organization will be focused. And what the leader focuses on the organization will focus on. If the leader focuses on his or her people, then the people will focus on people—people inside the organization as well as people outside the organization, such as clients and the community.

Not everyone is a leader. A person has to accept the responsibility of leadership to start to become a leader. Leaders are first and foremost responsible for the people they lead. That responsibility has to be accepted in order to be a leader.

The leader's passion is what helps create the inspiration in the people they lead. Leaders communicate their passion very well. That passion attracts people who are inspired and who become committed.

What's a No Matter What in your life? When you determine what that is, you gain clarity, and that allows you to focus on moving forward.

The power of commitment, No Matter What, will free you and empower you. No Matter What will change your life.

Chapter 1

COMMITMENT TO THE TRUTH

Accountability and truth go together. Accountability and lying never go together. Lack of truth, fake news, and alternative facts are flooding us. This barrage of false information has eroded accountability in our society.

You cannot have accountable people unless there is a foundation of truth. That "truth" for an individual is defined by our values and reflected in our character. As people, we become known for our character.

Truth is a whole lot deeper than the facts in a situation.

Just like an individual's truth is defined by his or her values, the "truth" inside of an organization is defined by the organization's set of values. The values become the standard, the foundation, by which everyone in the organization is living. The values establish the boundaries. They say, "This is how we do it here. This is our truth."

When there is a lack of truth, it shows up in both lies and deception. While both of these are negative and destroy accountability, there is a difference between the two.

Truth is deeper than facts.

People lie to keep themselves out of trouble. Children sometimes say that they did their homework, even though they did not do it, so they will not get punished. People inside of an organization may lie to buy time. They may say that something is done even though it has not been completed, thinking that they will get the task done before anyone discovers their neglect.

No one telling a lie ever thinks they are going to get caught in a lie. But they do.

Lies are only part of deception. Deception is dark, manipulative, and lacks transparency. Someone deceiving someone else is trying to get something that should not be theirs. There is no scenario where deception is good.

Deception is focused on trying to get someone to do something. There is a manipulation that is taking place. This can be a much more sinister situation than simply lying. When a person tries to get someone else fired so he or she can take the other person's job, deception is taking place. When people are being manipulated and an end goal is in play for the person who is deceiving everyone else, then that is deception.

Lying is about covering your tracks. Deception involves manipulation and some sort of personal gain. And both destroy accountability. There can be no accountability if lying or deception is present. It is scientifically impossible.

In other words, accountability cannot happen without the truth.

You have to have a foundation on what is true, right, and just. You also, at all times, have to live that foundation that you have proclaimed is true. And in addition to that, in every situation you must tell the truth.

Accountability cannot happen without the truth.

We want the truth to be on our own terms, but it just is not. The truth is the truth. We cannot decide what is true. We can and must live and tell the truth and, when we do that, we become known for being a person of truth. Being a person of truth becomes a significant part of how our character is defined.

Exaggeration is a lack of truth. It is a non-truth. In other words, exaggeration is lying. Now you may not be intending to deceive people, but if it is not true then it has to be a lie. There is no middle ground. There is no gray area. There is only black and white. There is truth, and there are lies. You choose which to live in your life. You choose your foundation, and ultimately you become known for what you stand for.

How do you find your foundation? This is a timeless question that has been asked millions of times throughout history. One time, the evening before a speech of mine had been scheduled, some of the leaders of the organization invited me to dinner with them. During the dinner I gave them an overview of what I was going to be discussing the following day in my presentation. We talked about values, non-negotiables, and, of course, accountability. I will never forget one of the people who sat at the table. His name is Larry. Larry was facing some challenges in his business, and I addressed them. I spoke to the values that he lived his life by and used as the basis for running his company. Then Larry asked a question that I did not expect. He asked, "What if you do not know what you believe?"

That question haunted me then, and it haunts me to this day. It haunted me because it had not crossed my mind that there are people, lots of people, who do not have clarity in what they believe. I struggled and did a lousy job of answering the question in the moment.

Since that time I have spent endless hours contemplating that question, thinking about my life and how I came to hold the set of beliefs that I have. If I were answering that question today, I would say that it is critical that we set aside the time to think about what we believe. We must be purposeful in our thoughts and reflections.

For most of us, our belief system and foundation starts in the teachings of our parents and other adults in our lives. Over time we take on the responsibility to determine just what foundation we want to build our life on. Through our life we are impacted through three opportunities: experiences, events, and evidence.

Experience is simply what we have encountered in our life and the lessons we learn from those experiences. Events may include events in our lifetime or those that happened in the past. The Holocaust is an event from which we can draw to determine what is right and wrong. The civil rights movement in the 1950s, 1960s, and beyond is an event filled with teachings for us to draw from. And there is evidence we discover in our life that following a specific believe system helps us move in the direction we want to go.

This is a personal journey and one filled with opportunities to connect with the values that we can live out in our life.

There has to be a consistency in testing your foundation. What you do consistently delivers a result. If I run five days a week, then over time I gain fitness, speed, and the ability to perform in road races at a competitive level. Making decisions consistently with your foundation will, likewise, deliver a result. If you have the right foundation, that consistency will deliver a very positive result for you.

Transparency will exhibit truth. Accountability cannot be present without transparency. Transparency creates confidence, trust, and loyalty in people. Confidence shows up in people believing that they can do anything. This confidence is what helps separate high-performance organizations from ordinary ones. Trust builds relationships. Better relationships lead to better communication, increased teamwork, and superior cooperation. Ultimately, transparency leads to loyalty. People want to stay and be a part of something that is bigger than themselves. Loyalty produces greater efficiency, lower operating costs, and greater profitability inside of an organization.

In your personal life, loyalty produces friends and family who will always be by your side and who will always be accountable to you!

When my cousin was 19, he came to live with us. His situation at home was not good, and he needed to be in a place where he was loved, nurtured, and encouraged. My parents took him in and did just that. As my parents aged, my cousin was always there to lend a helping hand. Many years later, he still visits and has breakfast with my mother every

Saturday morning. There is a loyalty there that can never be broken. He has maintained an accountability to my mother and to us, his adopted siblings.

Truth lasts forever. You can depend on the truth because it does not change. You can depend on a culture where truth is consistently present. You cannot depend on a person who accepts less than the truth.

People who seek truth want only truth and do not want anything else around them. They don't want "BS." They are not afraid of being told the truth. They love the truth, and they don't want to associate with anything that is not the truth or with people who accept less than the truth.

What happens to people who don't want to hear the truth? What happens to their organization? What happens to people when they want their egos stroked?

What happens is that the view of the organization becomes distorted. The view of the company's people becomes distorted. The view of what their people can accomplish becomes distorted. There is a false picture of where they are individually and organizationally. This false picture leads to bad decisions, and those bad decisions lead to a less-than-favorable outcome. When people don't want to hear the truth, they inevitably lead themselves and the people around them in the wrong direction. This is a recipe for failure.

The truth produces something. It produces a freedom. We have all heard the expression, "The truth will set you free." This actually originates in the New Testament—John 8:32.

What does this mean? Free from what? What will that freedom allow you to do? What happens if you do not have that freedom?

The reality is that truth frees you to be you. The standard by which you live your life is the truth that guides you. You make your decisions based on this standard. You are free to move forward because you know how to make decisions, what your decisions are based on, and that the decisions you make, if based on your standard, will always be the right decision.

The truth produces a freedom.

Lies hold you back. The truth enables you to progress forward. Deception holds you back. The truth frees you. Truth is pure. The truth allows you to do what is right, treat people right, make the right decision, and create a place where you and the others around you want to be.

Lying changes you physically. The act of telling a lie can be seen in brain scans. Lying raises blood pressure and increases respiration and perspiration. A lie detector test gauges a physical change in your body. Those increases in blood pressure and respiration are not good. Lying is not good physically, and it certainly is not good emotionally. You are different because of that lie.

The same types of things happen to an organization's spirit when the truth is not present. The culture of an organization will be negatively impacted when it lacks truth, and it will be transformed for the better when it consistently hears the truth.

There is always an impact to the culture. The culture of an organization is either a culture by design or it is a culture by default. A culture based on truth creates truth. People respond differently when they are in a culture where truth is present versus one where lying and deception are present.

The leader of an organization has the ability to control this. The leader has the ability to stand up for the truth and eliminate those people who are not willing to honor the truth.

That is part of the leader's responsibility—to protect the culture by protecting the truth. Remember, the truth in an organization is defined by its values. Protecting the values protects the truth and the culture it creates.

The leader must protect the organization's culture by protecting the truth.

A commitment to the truth by an individual will produce integrity, character, and respect. The Greek philosopher Heraclitus said, "Character is destiny."[1] So, you

---

1 "Heraclitus," Wikiquote, last modified November 7, 2017, https://en .wikiquote.org/wiki/Heraclitus.

create your future through your character, and your character is created through truth. Truth will create a much different future for you than lying and deceit. Truth will produce a future filled with great relationships, meaning, and purpose.

It is not the truth simply because you believe it. Truth is truth. Seeking truth, teaching truth, and only telling the truth will produce something wonderful in your life. Committing to the truth, no matter what, is the first step to living an accountable life.

Chapter 2

COMMITMENT TO WHAT YOU VALUE

Values have power.

A value is something that is extremely important you. It is something that is so important that if you lost it, you would move heaven and earth looking for it. There is worth there. Your principles or standards of behavior—what is important in life—are encapsulated in your stated values.

The real value of something is contained in its ability to produce good. Our values can produce good in our life. An organization's values can produce good in the organization, in its people, and in the community where the organization does business. I say "can" because for a value to be ours and to produce good we have to live that value. It cannot be a wish or a dream. Our decisions must be based on the values we say we have. Our decisions must always, 100 percent of the time, be based on our values or they are not our values. Remember, a commitment is "No Matter What."

> **The real value of something is contained in its ability to produce good.**

Values do not pertain to things. Values pertain to people. Our values state and illustrate how we see, connect to, and treat people. It is through our values that we build the connective tissue between people; relationships are formed, and accountability is based on our values. Your beliefs can change; your values don't.

I had the opportunity to sit down with Paul Harpole, the mayor of Amarillo, Texas, and have a very meaningful conversation with him. We were discussing the difference between values and beliefs when the look in Paul's eyes deepened and he shared a very powerful moment with me.

Paul said, "I was raised as a Catholic in a family of nine kids. I went off in the Army and was put in the position of evacuating patients in Vietnam. I held tiny babies who were dead and others who were maimed for life. I had this challenge with my faith because our belief was that if you were not baptized, you would never see God."

Paul paused, and what he said started to sink in. I could hear the emotion in Paul's voice even though it had been many years since Paul had this experience. The power in the moment was so strong, and I was totally pulled into it.

Then he said, "That's what I was taught all through 12 years of Catholic school. It was crazy. This was pure stupidity. How would God create this creature that would never ever see him because somebody didn't say the right words and sprinkle water on their heads? I said, 'That's stupid.' So I started challenging some really deeply held beliefs that I held because I was faced with holding a dying child. And then you apply that to other parts of your life and say, 'You can't make these stark judgments.'"

It was in this moment that Paul lost his man-made belief. That is when he began challenging all of his man-made beliefs.

I left that conversation emotionally moved. I connected to the immense strain that Paul must have been under in those moments of holding those babies. It made me question and think about things I may have been told that I wanted to make sure for myself were true or not. A child listens to what they are told, but as an adult I realized it was my responsibility to understand what is true and what is not.

Following that experience I sat down and scrutinized my personal beliefs, my values, and how all of them were formed. I wanted to know that what I believed wasn't just man-made to serve someone's purpose but was based in truth. I revisited my values because I strive to live them consistently in my life.

Many years prior to speaking with Paul I had spent considerable time reflecting on my values. I went through a series of exercises that I designed for myself and then began using with my clients. Ultimately, I identified three specific values. Those values are integrity, respect, and significance. Over the years I have continuously revisited those values and refined what they mean to me as I search for the deepest possible meaning.

Here are those values as I see them:

INTEGRITY

I make decisions based on the belief that my word is my bond and doing what is right is always the right thing to do. I commit to this no matter what.

RESPECT

I see all people as equal. I value other people's opinions, appreciate their beliefs, and recognize the importance of their priorities.

SIGNIFICANCE

I create meaning in my life and the lives of the people around me. I look for ways to create significance for my family. I make the effort to get to know people. I look for potential in the people with whom I come in contact. I encourage people. I participate in my community and work to make a difference.

Life is an adventure. I actively live that adventure when I live with integrity, respect, and significance.

I personally do not want to have to hold a dying baby to rethink my beliefs. I am thankful for Paul sharing his story. I want to know my truths. My beliefs and my values are built on top of that. And above all, I want to live my beliefs and values, not just shout them from the rooftops as words that I think people want to hear.

Your beliefs can change; your values don't.

An organization's values tell everyone how they will act inside the walls of the organization. You, as a leader, cannot tolerate any action that goes against those values.

Leaders fully know that it is only because they are committed to the values first that they can expect the people they lead to live the values also.

Values must be clearly defined. Anyone coming to work at the organization must be able to have crystal clarity as to what the values are and what they mean. The values lay out how to treat each other, how to treat the customer, what integrity is, what is expected professionally, how to handle when you make a mistake, what the character of the organization and the individual should be, and how the organization is committed to helping in the community. The values do not just tell you how to do it; rather, they outline what is expected of everyone. The values create "your" truth.

At the core, leaders know that the values are all that they really have. The values are as unique as a fingerprint. Your values are the only thing that differentiates you from anyone else. Leaders are certain of where their values come from, and they are certain of what those values will produce.

When your values are based on a foundation so solid that it has never let you down, you do not deviate from it. Your commitment only gets stronger.

Being committed to the values and treating them as non-negotiables does not mean you do not have a tender heart. It just means that you are firm in your conviction of the importance of those values and what is produced when you always, consistently, and absolutely operate from those values.

A leader establishes the relationship with their people through the organizational values. Everything about a great set of values tells your people that they are important. When your people believe that you value them, they will move mountains to avoid letting you down, to produce, to be an important part of the team, and to strive to be better.

People can get a paycheck anywhere, but when you build meaningful relationships with your employees, then you will continuously attract and keep the best people. People will want to work where it is known that the culture is great. That great culture is produced through the values.

Over time you will be known as an organization that has the cream of the crop. How can you not dominate your industry when you have the best people?! These relationships are driven by the values.

True leaders do not change the culture; they transform it. They can come into an organization and totally make it something that is the envy of not only their industry, but all businesses. They do this through their commitment to the values.

It may not be an overnight transformation, but anything of any value is worth putting in the commitment and time to make it happen. You will never produce sustainable, demonstrable long-term results by acting in the short-term.

What does it produce when there is a group of people who are operating out of the same set of values? It produces engaged employees. They look at how to make a simple task easier. They continually have positive interactions with each other. They are involved in each other's lives. The values put people in a position to care about each other. When you care for someone, you look out for their best interests. You provide for them. You want to protect them.

Fully living the values is a commitment to the truth of who you are as an individual and as an organization. Your values state, "This is how we do it here." They do not say, "This is how we do it here some of the time, most of the time, or when it is convenient." A commitment is No Matter What, and a commitment to the values produces something special.

It is this environment that makes for a positive and rewarding family life. It is also this environment that makes for a positive and rewarding business life. The same principles apply in both our personal and professional lives. As a matter of fact, we should be living our values equally through both our personal and professional life. If we truly value something it does not matter if we are dealing with our spouse, our child, or the coworker in the cubical next to ours—we should be living those values in the same way.

Circumstances may change. Your values do not. It is not the values that make you successful or create that amazing culture you want in your organization. It is a commitment to those values, no matter what, that delivers on that possibility and promise.

Because an organization usually is made up of many people, it may seem difficult to live the values to the degree of No Matter What. But if the leader believes in the values and is willing to accept nothing less than a commitment to a standard, a "this is how we do it here," then that special environment is produced. There is no other way it can happen.

Most organizations are made up of a diverse group of individuals. There can be people from four different generations working side by side. You have to be able to hold diverse groups together within an organization. There is only one way to do that. Bring in all of the generational experts that you want, but if you want to connect people and build a team you need an environment where everyone is committed to the values.

The circumstances can change. The values do not.

There can be people from different countries, different cultures, different religious backgrounds, and different political views all in the same organization. The values are what all the people can come together on. It is the values that connect and hold them together. That is why the organizations who have clearly defined values that are lived, no matter what, by their employees are always at the top of the lists of the best places to work.

I have worked with multinational companies and have observed that although they had locations in different countries where the customs were different, when they talked about their values everyone could come to an agreement. It is great to watch an organization be able to make both easy and difficult decisions by focusing on what they have in common—the values.

I have friends from around the world who are also professional speakers and authors. I have observed different cultures firsthand. What I have experienced, however, is that we have similar values. We all believe the same things about how to treat people, care for people, and keep our commitments. That is what has drawn us together.

Determining your personal values may be the best single investment you can make in yourself. I have discovered that personal values connect to four specific areas:

1. **Foundational Values**—The basis or groundwork on which anything stands

2. **Relational Values**—The way in which two or more people behave toward and deal with each other

3. **Professional Values**—The manner in which you approach your career and calling

4. **Community Values**—How you feel about, participate in, and support your community

Think about your life experiences, reflecting on when you have felt good about your decisions and when you have not been happy with the choices you made. Then take the time to think about what you believe and your personal foundation. Now, in all of the four areas above, identify one or two values that have significance to you. Write down these values, but do not stop there. The next step is to define each value in detail as to what it means to you. It is this detailed definition that will guide you in your daily decisions and will determine what you can share with the people in your life.

Use this link to download our free *Discovering Your Values* **Worksheet:** **www.SamSilverstein.com/valuesworksheet.**

It is a little different with organizational values. The four types of values are the same but the application is to an organization versus an individual.

1. **Foundational Values**—What you stand for as an organization; the organization's character

2. **Relational Values**—How you treat and connect with people inside your organization as well as outside your organization

3. **Professional Values**—What level of excellence and performance is expected within the organization

4. **Community Values**—How you feel about, participate in and support your community

Go through the steps listed above to identify and define very specifically what your organizational values are.

In my book *Non-Negotiable,* I share the core values of Happy State Bank and Trust. When you look at their values, you will see that they connect very strongly with all four of these areas. That is what makes their values so good, so effective, and so powerful.

> **Use this link to download our free *Discovering Your Organizational Values* Worksheet: www.SamSilverstein.com/valuesworksheet.**

There is a difference between a policy in an organization and a value. I once had a client that wanted help articulating their values and establishing them inside their organization so that they would have the organizational culture that they really desired. We facilitated this process, and as we sat around the table and talked about their values, the president of the company said that community service was a value of theirs. He went on to say that it was so much of a value that in their policy manual it stated that all employees could have up to two days off with pay to perform community service.

My assistant, Sharon, asked the client how many days off with pay in order to perform community service had been recorded the prior year. After a little thought and checking with the bookkeeper, who was in the room, the answer was zero! There was silence in the room, which I broke with the statement, "Community Service is a policy for you. Let's make it a value." And that is what we did. They defined what community service was to them, articulated the importance to the organization, and delineated how the people could go about living that value.

Within a few short weeks, we started to hear stories about all of the community service their team members were providing. They were painting houses, helping the elderly, and even "adopting" a homeless family in transition from one part of the country to another to help them get home.

This is what happens when a policy becomes a value. To be a value it must be identified, understood, and lived. You have to see the value showing up in your life or in your organization for it really to be a value. When you live it, no matter what, it is a value.

Some organizations do OK without specifically defining their values, just as some people do OK without taking the time to define theirs. But all organizations and people will find greater clarity and direction and achieve at a higher level when they fully discover, define, and live their values.

When you take the time to discover and define your values, you create an inner peace. You have effectively made decisions in advance of any situation presenting itself. When you need to make a decision, all you have to do is live out your values.

Your values become the foundation for all action. And when you totally believe in your values, you know them, you live them, and you protect them. You never allow a

decision to be made that would take a value away from you.
You live your values No Matter What.

Chapter 3

COMMITMENT TO
"IT'S ALL OF US"

The word *help* means more than just "to assist." It also means "to lend strength." When you are lending strength to someone, you are putting forth a sincere effort to help them do what they are trying to do. A person feels different when someone is there to help them. Think about a time when someone stepped up and said, "Let me help you with that." It is as if they said, "I am on your side. You are not alone. We can do this together."

Just knowing that someone cares about you and your success makes you feel good. It makes you feel more capable.

It makes you feel like success is guaranteed. When some-one is helping you and you feel that they "have your back," a confidence grows within you that causes you to succeed, and it also causes you to want to avoid letting them down.

When someone cares enough to help you, it is done because of a relationship. The very action of someone help-ing another person is also an investment in a relationship, and that relationship grows.

When it comes to accountability, it is common to hear the expression, "I am going to hold you accountable." There is another way, a more powerful way, of looking at account-ability in a relationship, and that is, "I am going to help you be accountable." These are two very different perspectives on accountability in relationships.

I have always wondered why we use the word *hold* instead of *help* when referencing accountability. When you "hold" someone accountable, it is like you are forcing them to do something, and people do not respond to that. Helping someone is a whole other level of commitment. It is deeper. There is a different intent.

Hold is one-sided, and that one is you. *Help* is two-sided. You help them, and in the process you gain as well. There is a different relationship. It is a right relationship. This is a leadership relationship. Helping is what a leader does. Holding is the tactic of an authoritarian.

Everything connects back through relationships. Accountability is about relationships. Commitment is about relationships. Values connect people in deeper relationships. Through relationships you can accomplish a wondrous multitude of things.

Some people value relationships, and others do not. Some people only value a relationship where someone can do something for them. It is the real and sincere relationship that bonds people and sets the stage for shared and mutual success, happiness, and fulfillment.

Accountability is about relationships.

When someone commits to "It's all of us," they are committing to a rewarding relationship at the same time. They have an attitude of "We succeed together. We fail together. We are all on the journey together." They know that if you look good, you all look good. If you look bad, you all look bad. It is all or nothing. They are willing to connect with and support everyone in the process of building something that is bigger than they are.

The television show *Spartan: Ultimate Team Challenge* illustrates this perfectly. Teams of five people, including both men and women on the same team, compete over a grueling mile-long obstacle course. It takes strength, speed, determination, and grit to get through the course as a team. And you do not get credit for crossing the finish line until everyone on the team crosses the finish line. Everyone wins or no one wins at all.

I have noticed that different team members are better at different aspects of the course. Some are great climbers, and some are very strong. Some are big, and others are smaller. Some are the base of a human pyramid, and some are pushed to the top. Each person has a role. Separately, they could never finish the course; together, they move mountains.

Every team takes the attitude that "If someone slows down, we all slow down." It is the only way to keep the team together, to keep them at their strongest, and ultimately to have a chance at winning.

If you break your leg, your whole body hurts. Your whole body is sick and has to adjust. Similarly, when you face trouble as an organization, you all face it. When you celebrate your success, everybody celebrates.

When there is that kind of conscious mental thinking about your values, there is nothing you cannot do. You have to be committed to this way of thinking. It is not situational. It is all the time.

People know when they are a part of the whole. They know when the leader sees them as an integral part of this whole. When people feel like an important part of the team, they believe that they can do anything. This thinking impacts the work they take on, the challenges they are willing to face, and the risks they will take. People will get closer to the edge when they know that they are a part of the whole, and when that happens they achieve things they never would have tried otherwise.

When a leader commits to "It's all of us," they know that there is not a different standard for the leader and the person on the front line. Everyone lives the values.

What do you do when someone goes rogue? You try and coach them up, but some people will not change. If someone is not committed to "It's all of us," then you have to get them off the team. They should no longer be a part of "all of us."

As an organization, you have to know what you believe about your people. Most people think they know what they believe about their people, but I do not think they really do. Their actions tell me otherwise.

Leaders that determine the ability and potential of an individual based on their level of education, the school they went to, and other extraneous items will always be limiting their people. If you are narrow-minded in how you look at people, you will never believe and commit to "It's all of us." You will always be breaking out groups of people as "better than" and "less than."

Sometimes we see someone who dresses differently or who has tattoos, multiple piercings, or other visual differences, and we make a judgment about that person. That type of thinking is close-minded. If we see people as different, then we can't commit to "It's all of us."

How we see people is critical to a richness of life and the success of an organization that wants accountability to be at the very heart of what they are.

Prejudice, bias, and stereotyping can sneak up on people. It is not that a leader meant to put a ceiling on his people based on their level of formal education, but many times they do and they do not even know it.

We say things before we even realize what we are saying. We comment about people and we do not even know their stories. We judge people based on what we think we know. When we do that, nine times out of ten we are wrong.

I was about to walk into a restaurant one time when a lady and her young son hurriedly approached the building. I held the door for them as they drew near. When they walked in, I heard the mom say to her son, "That's OK. We're only two minutes late." I thought to myself, "Wow, this mom is teaching her son that being a few minutes late is OK. If two is OK, maybe five is also?" Well, guess what? I just passed judgment. I do not know their story. I do not know where they are coming from, why they are late, or the events of their day. Maybe they had just been to the doctor and the mom was trying to console and relax her son.

Some people are more talkative and some are quieter and harder to get to know. We need to know people and understand their story so we can help them, not judge them.

Many organizations focus on how their employees are going to treat the customers and fail to focus on how they are going to treat each other. It is critical to attend to how people inside an organization are going to relate, communicate, and build relationships. When you figure that part out, building relationships with customers comes much easier. If your people know how to build relationships internally, they will naturally build relationships externally.

Companies that focus on customer service and are not first committed to how their people are treated will forever come up short and be looking for the next customer service consultant to try and solve their problems. On the other side of the coin, when I see organizations where customers are not treated great, I know that the people inside the organization are not treated great.

How you communicate can either be inclusive or exclusive. When only certain individuals are privy to information, people feel excluded and left out. While there can be some sensitive information that needs to be restricted, there is far less than many leaders think.

Leaders would be amazed at the solutions that their people could create if the people had access to information. Involving everyone in the conversation provides better, faster, and more diverse solution ideas to challenges. The transparency you achieve by sharing information, good or bad, enables you to continue to build trust. It is through this trust that people come to believe that their company's attitude is "It's all of us." When your people feel this way, it leads to loyalty.

"It's all of us" is all about unity, relationships, being a team, and treating each other with mutual respect. "It's all of us" recognizes that we are all different, but we connect through the values. It is the view that together, we will succeed.

Transparency in leadership creates trust and loyalty.

If you want to make it about all of us, you should stop and take stock of how you think. People need to pay attention to what they think about. That is where the judgment shows up. Do you recognize when you have judgmental thoughts? Do you allow those thoughts to stay? Do you attempt to change? Having an "It's all of us" mind-set means slowing down and realizing what you are thinking, saying, and doing. When you make a conscious effort to monitor your thoughts to see where your thinking is limiting how you see people and then work hard to make changes, you are taking steps in the right direction to being a better person and a better leader.

You can always tell how you think by looking at how you act. Your actions are the leading indicators to what you believe and think.

At some level people have to make a conscious decision to change in order to believe that "It's all of us." It takes time to change. You may have to be vulnerable. You may need to uncover something about yourself that you don't like and then work to change that.

It starts with stopping and asking yourself, "Where am I coming up short? How can I be better? What do I need to improve about myself?"

When your actions tell me "It's all of us," then I not only feel like I am a part of something important, something bigger than me, but I also learn the importance of helping others. I learn what happens when we work together. I begin to value and appreciate that we all go there together or we do not go at all. When that is the prevailing attitude in an organization, people pull together in a way that would otherwise not be possible. "It's all of us" becomes the desired and appreciated way of doing things for everyone.

Chapter 4

COMMITMENT TO STAND WITH YOU WHEN ALL HELL BREAKS LOOSE

All the events in our life are not going to be smooth and rosy. Sure, most of what we experience in life can be grand and beautiful, but we are also going to run into challenges. Living life sometimes is literally moving from one difficult event to another and managing these challenging situations.

In an organization it can be the same way. Things happen at every business. Things happen that are man-made, and things happen that are not. We face crises, issues, and change. Change happens every single day.

Stuff is going to happen. The question is, how are you going to react to it?

It is how you are reacting to what is going on that becomes the issue. Sometimes there are internal factors, and sometimes there are external factors. Sometimes you can control things, and sometimes you cannot. The one thing you can control is how you react. The only thing we can truly control in this world is our attitude at any given moment.

When I was the president of the National Speakers Association, my very close and dear friend Phillip Van Hooser was the president-elect. During the board meetings he always sat on my right. Meetings went smoothly, and I enjoyed the privilege and honor of serving as president. Most of the time I was calm and let my calmness be part of the way I led. But there were some issues that really caused my passion to surface. Once in a while, I would become more excited, and that excitement impacted the mood in the room.

Phil was always there to let me know, either with a glance or a pat, when I was getting a bit overexcited. Phil had my back. He was with me no matter what, and knowing that I had his support meant the world to me.

My goal as the leader was to prepare him in every way I could and to include him in important conversations so that his presidency would go smoothly. And as someone who fully understands leadership, he was there, no matter what, to help me be the best leader I could be. His greatest gift was the reminder of the power of staying calm in the most trying of moments.

In an organization, if the leadership stays focused and calm, so does everyone else. If the leadership loses control, so does everyone else. If what you believe and value produces a positive result, then staying steady with those values during times of change and challenge will guide you through. It takes a lot of guts to stick to what you value, but when you are committed to standing with someone when all hell breaks loose, those values are what ground you.

People think that change is bad, or that it is going to affect their paycheck or their livelihood, or that they are going to have to change how they do something. The truth is that when you get bogged down in that sort of thinking, you get left behind.

As soon as you stand in the way of change, you get run over. Embracing change allows you to speed ahead.

And then there is the trauma that can be caused by change. There is internally driven change as well as externally driven change, and both types, when not handled correctly, can cause stress. But it does not have to be that way.

You could decide to redesign your sales procedures. That would be internal change. The government could make changes in laws or compliance issues. That would be external change. Your best producer gets sick, and you have more internal change. The stock market goes crazy, and a little external change is shoved your way. It's going to happen regularly, and we need to accept that reality of life.

Embracing change allows you to speed ahead.

Change does not have to be bad. It can be good. It can be great. Any advancement in technology, quality of life, and betterment of people or organizations always comes through change. Actually, for those people and organizations that really understand change, change is just a decision.

The reason that change is nothing but a decision for some organizations is that the leader is systematic with the *what*, *why*, and *how* of change. They do this through their values. It is incumbent on the leader to connect the values to these three specific pieces of information so that the people they lead will understand and embrace the change.

So now it really is just a decision that needs to be made. The Terms of Change™ are simply that *what*, *why*, and *how*.

We all communicate differently, and we all need different information to process change in an efficient and relaxed manner. Some people just need to know *what* the change is in order to get on board and move forward with the change. It really can be that simple for them.

There are other people who need to know *why* we are changing. They want that explanation and information in order to process the change properly. Once they have the *why* they are ready to move forward.

Then there are the *how* people. These people want the details of how the change is going to be implemented and handled and what the next steps are. With the *how* information in hand, they are ready to accept the change.

There is a fourth group of people when it comes to change. They ask a lot of questions. They seem to rebuff change. They seem to be against leadership at every turn. We call them troublemakers! The reality is that these people are *what*, *why*, and *how* people. That's right—they need all three pieces of information to process change. Once they have this information, they not only come alongside the decision to change, but many times they end up being the biggest and most vocal supporters of the change.

It is always your responsibility as a person leading change in your personal life or in your business to supply all of this information up front. Do not wait for someone to ask those questions. If you provide the information proactively then you are being transparent and people will trust and respect you. This builds relationships and speeds up the change process. When someone has to ask questions to get all of the information, they think you are holding back and that there is a downside to the change of which you do not want them aware.

Change becomes just a decision because you have provided all of the information that people need to accept, embrace, and make change happen.

Beyond change, there are times when things are just going to go wrong. Equipment is going to fail. People make mistakes. Some leaders look to blame rather than stand by someone. This is where the relationship factor comes into play. When you take the time to build relationships, you protect those relationships by standing with someone when all hell breaks loose.

Blame can be a really ugly thing inside of an organization, or inside of a family, or inside of a government. Blame is at the opposite end of leadership. When we blame someone, it is a deficiency in us.

Blame causes division inside of any organization. Blame causes shame. Blame causes people to take sides. Blame tears relationships apart. Blame erodes "It's all of us." It creates chaos. It spawns the kind of chatter you do not want inside of an organization. President Abraham Lincoln got it right when he said, "A house divided against itself cannot stand."[1]

Blame destroys loyalty, trust, and the desire to work together. A leader owns the situation, especially if it's bad.

---

1 Abraham Lincoln, "House Divided Speech," Springfield, Illinois, June 16, 1858. *Abraham Lincoln Online*, http://www .abrahamlincolnonline.org/lincoln/speeches/house.htm.

Leaders recognize that mistakes will be made. It serves no purpose to blame someone. You need to figure out and fix what went wrong so it doesn't happen again. You may have to let someone go over what went wrong. There is difference between a mistake and something that happened intentionally. It is up to leadership to know the difference and to act in an appropriate manner.

A leader owns the situation, especially if it's bad.

When most people hear the phrase "The buck stops here," they think of President Harry S. Truman. President Truman had a sign on his desk with that statement on it. As a leader, you take the responsibility when something is not working or goes sour. You help your people solve the problem, you do not dish out blame, and you move on.

All hell can break loose in your personal life as well as in your business. It can happen very quickly and without any warning.

One of my daughter's closest friends was at work in a neighboring city when she found out that her older brother had suddenly passed away. Death is traumatic at any age, but when you are in your twenties it just doesn't make sense. My daughter's friend made quick plans to get back to St. Louis to be there with her parents and to prepare for the funeral. When she was leaving work that day, her boss asked, "When are you coming back to work?"

A true leader would have recognized the crisis and would have stood by her. He would have supported her in any way necessary. He would have driven her across the state to get home if that was what was needed. Instead, when a crisis hit, he thought of his own needs, and he abandoned her. This is not leadership.

Leadership shows up when the tough decisions have to be made. It's not the title that makes a leader.

Leaders never look to offload a problem or issue onto someone else. They build loyalty because the people they lead know that they will always stand by their followers. This is why people want to serve a true leader.

> **Leadership shows up when the tough decisions have to be made.**

Leadership is a responsibility, and it is not always glamorous. It means taking the bad with the good. You give credit for the success to those around you who really did make it happen, and you take responsibility for the failure because you could have trained someone better, supported someone better, or helped someone to better handle the situation.

Assessing what went wrong does not mean you are engaging in blame. Professional sports teams analyze their performance after every single game. They review video of the game and look for ways to improve. This process is about always trying to get better. Correcting what needs to be corrected can be done without making someone feel shame and like it is their fault. You can grow your people as you grow your systems and organization.

You can build someone up even though they screwed up. Doing this creates a situation where they will not want to let you down next time. They also will be better focused as a result and will be loyal to you as their leader.

Throughout this entire process you are building relationships. Relationships are a key ingredient of accountability. As I've mentioned before, a person will never be accountable to someone with whom they do not have a relationship.

This is how effective leaders act, and because they act a certain way, there are going to be positive outcomes inside of the organization.

A commitment to "stand with you when all hell breaks loose" gives everyone around you the assurance that you are with them in good times and bad times, that they are safe even if they mess up, and that you will support learning, fixing, and growing through the process.

Chapter 5

COMMITMENT TO THE FAULTS AND FAILURES AS WELL AS THE OPPORTUNITIES AND SUCCESSES

This commitment is all about the character of an individual. This is about overlooking other people's faults and failures. I overlook your faults and failures because I have them too. Everybody has faults and failures.

If I am a true leader, then I am going to focus more on your successes. That is what should really count to me.

Leaders see the good in people. Leaders see the contributions their people have made and the contributions they have the potential to make.

This is all about honesty and authenticity. First, you must be honest with yourself. You admit your own faults. If you expect more from someone else than from yourself, you have a problem.

> **True leaders focus more on people's successes.**

Then, you are authentic with others. When you are authentic and real and honest about your own faults, it naturally attracts others to you. This is the mark of a great person, and this is the mark of a great leader, the kind of person that other people will want to follow and support. We do not have to be perfect to be wonderful.

Some leaders want to appear to be perfect. Because no one is perfect, no one is going to ever relate to someone who positions themselves as perfect. I have seen this with friends, I have seen it with corporate executives with whom I have worked, and I have seen it with our nation's leaders. When you share your faults, you create a safe place for others to admit their faults and shortcomings.

It is easy to fall into the trap of being judgmental and finding everyone else's faults. I fall into that trap way more than I would like. After I go down that hole, I wake up and realize that I am not in a place I want to be. I hate it when this happens and, quite honestly, I start kicking myself for allowing it to happen.

A fault is whatever impairs excellence.

I do not really care to hang out with people who are always judging others, and I certainly do not want to be that person myself—but it happens. What I have discovered is that when I live with gratitude, then I see people differently. I see the best in people and do not focus on their faults. And when I stop pretending that I never make a mistake or do things the wrong way, I also discover the great things that the people around me do. For me, this is a habit I work to develop. I know I am not completely there, but I am working hard to keep improving.

A fault is whatever impairs excellence. It is an imperfection.

My daughter Allison broke her leg in two places playing soccer. They had to put a couple of pins in when they set the bones. Allison has a great attitude. We were talking about the scar on her ankle one day, and I was concerned about how she was going to feel about having it. Allison immediately pointed out a few other little scars that she has. She was proud of her scars. She said, "Scars tell a story about your life."

Your scars, your "imperfections," tell a story about you. The "story" from your imperfections is what you have learned, and what you have learned makes you better. Every person has imperfections, and every organization has them also. You can learn from your mistakes. When you focus on learning from your mistakes, you grow and get better. Who does not want to be better?

Acknowledging someone else's faults to feel better about ourselves or to deny our faults is destructive. It does not build a relationship. It tears one down. We all know people who are very judgmental. When we are judgmental, we are using someone else's faults to try to deny or justify our own. Being judgmental is not really about the person we are judging; it is about us trying to feel better at someone else's expense.

There is something so very positive about a leader who is always visible no matter how tough the situation. Many leaders get it backward. Real leaders are out there when times are tough, and when success is what everyone sees they are back behind the people, putting them out there in the spotlight. True leaders have the shoulders to carry the faults and the blame. They have the heart to make sure their team gets recognized for the successes.

Leaders are quick to point out their shortcomings and even quicker to see and acknowledge the strengths and contributions of everyone around them. This all flows from how leaders see their people.

Because no one is perfect, we all make mistakes. Sometimes these mistakes lead to a poor outcome. The focus should never be on perfection. Rather, it should always be on excellence. Excellence is achieved through a mind-set of, "How can I do this better?" When you continuously ask this question, you are always going to get an answer as to how to improve.

As a professional speaker, I record every speech I give, and someone reviews it with me with only one question in play: "How can I do this better?" My goal is that no matter how good a speech might be, I want it to be better the next time.

Before I began writing this book, my assistant, Sharon, asked me, "What are you going to do differently this time that is going to allow you to write it better?" Sharon was not saying that my last book was not good. We want to achieve excellence, and we know the only way to do so is to ask this question and strive to always improve.

Celebrate when good things happen. When you celebrate someone else, you not only recognize their achievements, but you also show through your actions just how important they are. Celebrating builds relationships.

Leaders allow their people to have opportunities and successes in their careers. Sometimes in an organization a person will come forward with an idea of something new that could be done inside of their business or organization. A great leader will recognize a valid idea and then will allow that person to effectively create that new position and then run with that opportunity.

Sometimes an employee goes to an employer and says, "I think there is a better way to do this." You may not believe it, but there are some employers who will say, "Just go do your job." Talk about a demotivated employee! When a leader respects people, takes the time to listen, and then allows that person to implement their ideas, a powerful moment in the life of that employee occurs. They are given an opportunity for success. That employee will reward the leader with supreme dedication and a full commitment to their relationship.

Successes can also be about things that happen in people's families. That is right: you can celebrate at work, as an organization or department, something that an individual or a person's family achieved. Maybe someone earned a degree in their spare time. Or maybe someone's son or daughter accomplished something. Everyone can come together to celebrate those successes.

Promotions within a company can be celebrated. Something as simple as reducing the cost of manufacturing by five cents apiece could be celebrated.

Celebrations give you the opportunity to show appreciation and support. Celebrating brings out the best in people, and it makes them want to work to achieve additional success just so you can celebrate again.

In my younger days, when I went to camp, we had to clean our cabin every day. Every day when we were out at activities, someone would come into the cabin and score how good of a job we did. The cabin with the highest score each day received a popsicle party. We all celebrated our success, and we were all motivated to go do it again.

Well, it's the same thing inside of an organization or a family. Celebrate with your spouse and children at every opportunity. You will be recognizing their achievements individually and the achievements of the family collectively, and you will also be teaching your children, through example, to live a life filled with celebrations for not only their achievements but the achievements of the people around them. In the process, they will come to know just how much they mean to you, how important they are.

When the people around you know that you are committed to the entire experience, the faults and failures as well as the opportunities and successes, you stand taller in their eyes. You are contributing to your relationship with them. You are telling them, "I am with you. We are together in this."

People feel relaxed and safe in that environment. They are able to focus because they know you have their back. This creates loyalty. It bonds you together. They also know that it is OK not to hit the bull's eye every time. Failure is not failure. Failure becomes a learning experience.

Failure is connected to a timeline. What is failure right now could be success by tomorrow. Just because you have not yet achieved your goal does not mean you will not achieve your goal. Maybe you just need to try again. It is only failure when you quit, and you are less likely to quit when you know someone has your back.

It is that commitment to trying again that becomes contagious. Leaders set the example, and their team carries that attitude forward in intent, effort, and then in result.

When everyone in your life or your organization is linked through the faults and failures as well as the opportunities and successes, you all share a common bond. You are connected. You trust each other. Your commitments to each other mean something very important, and you never want to let anyone around you down.

Chapter 6

COMMITMENT TO SOUND FINANCIAL PRINCIPLES

A commitment to sound financial principles will impact your life and the lives of the people around you. Without a commitment to sound financial principles you may very well not be able to live the life you want, deserve, and desire. Without this commitment you may not be able to bless other people with your generosity. There is a stability in your life that a commitment to sound financial principles brings.

Everyone is not at the same place in life. We all have different opportunities and are faced with different challenges.

Some of us were gifted with a great education. Others of us came from troubled families and weak financial situations. No matter your background or where you are currently, you can improve your situation. You can transform your life. You can make a difference not only in your situation, but in the situations of the people around you.

I know that I was very fortunate growing up. My parents started with very little but worked hard to save, start a business, and create financial success in their lives. What I was blessed to experience was not just how they modeled hard work and the desire to save, but I watched them give, make a difference in organizations they believed in, and show up in people's lives who needed someone at a critical point in time and help them. I benefitted from their labors, but I also learned so much from the example they set on how they gave and made a difference.

My parents took into our home or provided for at least three of my cousins. Two of them lived in our house for an extended period of time. My parents "rescued" another, a first cousin once removed, and supported him in a boarding school that allowed him to mature and discover himself.

At my father's funeral, someone approached me to tell me what my parents meant to him and how they totally changed the direction of his life. It was this young man, now grown with a family of his own, for whom my parents had made a difference. I was able to witness firsthand my parents achieve success financially and also see how they shared that financial success in the service of others.

For some it may take more time and more hardship. For others it may take more discipline. For others it may take a change in the way you think and how you live.

Below are ten financial principles that have proven themselves over generations. They apply to us individually, and they apply to businesses and organizations. You may start with one or two and work up to all ten, or you may be able to implement all ten right now. Whatever your situation, know that herein lies the secret for sound financial principles, and you can do it.

GIVE

Giving is essential to sound financial principles. I know, you are thinking, "I'm trying to gain wealth, not give it away." The truth is that giving causes several things to happen.

If you believe that what you give comes back, then giving reinforces your faith in that belief. The act of giving aligns with what you say you believe. Giving also is an investment in your spirit, in your well-being, and in other people. Investing in other people is just as important as investing in yourself.

Giving is an investment in your spirit, in your well-being, and in other people.

We have to decide what "stuff" means to us. We have to decide if stuff is more important to us or if people are more important to us. What you give will make a difference for someone, and making a difference is important. I believe that we are here to make a difference in the world. When we give, we have the opportunity to do just that.

One way to look at money is through the lens of stewardship versus ownership. Do you own the money you have, or are you a steward of the money? The answer to that question will dramatically change how you think, act, and make decisions about the money. If you feel that you absolutely own it, you earned it all yourself, it was solely your efforts, then you may spend it one way. When you believe that you own it, then when you give it you may have ego attached to that gift, and you may require something of the recipient in the form of shown appreciation.

If, on the other hand, you see that money as something that you worked hard for but not something earned entirely by you, if you believe that the money was put in your hands with a duty and you have a responsibility to steward that money for a greater good, then you will use, invest, and give the money another way. If you believe that what you have came from a higher being, and that your duty is to make a difference with it, things change. This broader view of wealth, its origin, and its purpose will motivate you to act differently with it.

When you realize that what we have was given to us, then giving takes on an entirely new level of responsibility.

Giving becomes part of who you are. Giving is so important that you will even sacrifice in order to give. Sacrificing in order to give is a natural act that permeates our being. Just because you give does not mean you sacrifice. Do not confuse the two. Every gift does not have to be a sacrifice, but making a sacrifice in order to give takes that gift to a whole new level.

When you are a giver, you cannot help it. It is what you believe that you are supposed to do. It is who you are.

A while back, my assistant, Sharon, was diagnosed with chronic kidney failure. Our insurance sees many expenses as "non-medical," such as the many trips from Amarillo to a hospital in Oklahoma City that Sharon had to take. When the people at Happy State Bank in Amarillo heard about Sharon's condition, they came together to raise a substantial amount of money to assist in those expenses. Sharon is not used to receiving; she is used to giving. Not accepting the money was not an option when they presented their gift to her. Their gracious giving made a significant difference for Sharon.

This all may sound well and good, but you need to understand that while there was a relationship in place with Pat and the team at Happy State Bank, Sharon did not bank there. Sharon did not have an account at the bank, but that did not matter. It did not matter to them because they believe in giving at every opportunity. They believe that it is their responsibility, purpose, and mission to give. They believe that their creator expects that of them. And they give without ever expecting anything in return.

BE THANKFUL

Thank the source of your well-being. Thank the source of what comes your way. If you think your boss is the source of your portion, then thank her. If you think your customers are your source, then by all means thank them. If you think God is the source, then most certainly say thanks. Do not ignore your source. Say thank you often.

Gratitude will change the way you see everyone and everything. It will change the way you see money and possessions. Your appreciation for those people in your life who help you reach your financial goals will change when you live a life of gratitude and thankfulness.

It is easier to focus on what bothers us rather than what is actually working for us. Operating from a position of gratitude will impact our thinking and ultimately our doing.

HAVE A FINANCIAL PLAN

Very rarely do things happen by accident. The most successful people I know plan their success by thinking and designing a specific course of action to take. A financial plan will help you do that.

There are all kinds of financial plans. Some are very complex, and some are quite simple. I saw one recently that was made up of five buckets into which you divide your monthly income. They are:

1. Donate

2. Give

3. Save

4. Invest

5. Spend

The plan went on to illustrate that:

- We should donate 10 percent of our income to our synagogue, church, temple, mosque, or other spiritual place we associate.

- We should give 10 percent to our community where need is present.

- Our savings should be 10 percent so we are prepared for a rainy day.

- Investments should make up 20 percent of our income. These investments will grow and produce a future income.

- And of course that leaves 50 percent to spend.

I realize that not everyone has the disposable income that far exceeds what they need for food, shelter, clothes, and other essentials, but seeing these five buckets in action makes sense. And I'm not saying that this is the plan to follow. I am saying that sticking to a clear plan in which you sacrifice will yield results.

Your plan is certainly personal to you. No matter what your plan is, I would encourage you to be purposeful. When you make decisions intentionally with all the facts, you receive a specific result for a reason.

All of the buckets above make a lot of sense. There is a return from assigning money to each of those areas. I have already addressed the importance of giving. Think about this plan, or create one of your own. No matter what, create and implement a financial plan in your life.

WORK HARD

You have to do more than just show up. Everybody shows up. Do more than that. It is important to understand the value of what you do in order to be fully committed and to give your best effort in your work. Every job has value to someone. A janitor sweeping the floor creates a cleaner and safer work environment for the people who work in that area.

You are not only working hard for yourself; you are working hard for the people around you. Your hard work is not just based on getting things done. It is based on service to others. When you serve others diligently, you provide greater value, you build relationships, and you create loyalty. Just as a business that provides better service to its customers has a greater chance to flourish, so does a person who provides a greater service to the people around them, both inside and outside of their place of work. The service you provide others matters to them. It should matter to you too.

Serve unselfishly, without expectation of anything in return. Through an attitude of service you meet new people and your sphere of relationships expands. People want to do business with people they know and like. People will present opportunities to others whom they know and like. Your next opportunity could come from someone new to whom you provide a service today.

It is also important to work honestly. How you come by your wealth, no matter how great or small that wealth is, is important. No great long-term success can come from less-than-honorable actions. A quick profit or gain at someone else's expense breaks all the laws of life, and there will be consequences. It is better to lose money on a deal honorably, no matter how much it hurts, than to make money dishonorably.

SAVE

Saving for tough times and for our future is critical. Many times we put off saving because we think that we will earn more money in the future and saving will be easier. Using a realistic interest rate, that dollar you save today will grow into 5 dollars in 20 years, 11 dollars in 30 years. If you put a few zeros behind the dollar, think of what can happen!

Sometimes people think that if they cannot save something substantial then it is not worth saving at all. That is just wrong. The best savers I know always started by saving pennies before they built up to saving dollars.

I was walking into a store one day when a few kids walked out. They must have been barely old enough to drive. The young man had a bag in one hand with his recent purchase. His other hand was clinched in a fist. I watched as he opened his hand to reveal some change. He looked at it, thought for a second, and then threw the change down on the ground. It meant nothing to him.

I have a friend who put a water jug out and any time she had spare change she dropped it in the jug. One day she needed some money. There was over 100 dollars in the water jug. Pennies add up quickly.

At a church that a friend of mine attends they needed to raise money for an organization that helps mothers and babies. The church bought boxes of baby bottles, passed them out, and asked people just to fill it with their change and bring it back by a certain date. They raised thousands of dollars. Pennies, nickels, dimes, and quarters add up!

The key to saving is not necessarily the amount; it is the consistency. If you just take five dollars out of your check each week, that will add up over time. Start with something.

LIVE BELOW YOUR MEANS

It is better to pretend to be poor than to pretend to be rich. When you act like you have more than you do, you tend to buy things you should not, you might waste money, and you can run up all kinds of interest and debt that, one day, you will have to repay. It also shows a lack of gratitude for what you really do have. Remember the be thankful thing? When we try to live a lifestyle beyond our means, it ends up costing us, both today and in the future.

When you live below your means, you position yourself to save, invest, give, and create a future filled with possibilities for you and the people around you. We may need everything we have just to survive. I fully understand that, but I am always moved by people who find a way to look a little "poorer" than they really are, and they are not worried about what other people think about their material possessions.

> It is better to pretend to be poor than to pretend to be rich.

My parents' goal was always to create a better life for us, their children, than they had. They lived well below their means so that they could afford for us to get the best possible education and be positioned to provide for our kids an even better life. As I grew older, I discovered that their parents had lived their lives with the same mantra of wanting a better life for their children, my parents, than they had themselves. Imagine the impact of several generations living in a way to ensure that the next generation has it better—better education, better quality of life, better opportunities.

Reach for the best, but also plan for the worst. Even when things are going well, events can happen that cause financial challenges. By living below your means, you position yourself to plan for the eventual economic downturn, medical emergency, or unexpected expenditure that pops up in your life.

BE DEBT FREE

Borrowing money that you absolutely do not need will enslave you, not enrich you. When you borrow money for things you do not really need, be it a nicer car, bigger home, or whatever, you not only have to pay back the principal, but you have to pay back the interest as well. The more you pay out, the less you have to save, invest, or give to a worthy cause.

Yes, most of us must borrow money to buy a house. Beyond that, once you eliminate debt from your life you create a way of life where everything costs you less. It costs less because you are paying for only the item. Tack on interest, and many times you end up actually paying three or four times the original cost. That is an expensive and inefficient way to live.

BE CONTENT

Learning to put off gratification will add greatly to one's inner peace and also to one's long-term financial net worth. I'm always excited when I hear a news story about a school teacher on a modest income who dies and leaves several million dollars to charity. The way that happens is because the individual learns to be content with what they have. They do not need something else to find personal satisfaction and happiness. Actually, they discover that things do not bring happiness. Relationships and shared experiences bring happiness.

That money you do not spend today by not having to have the latest, newest, fanciest, or most popular item will be money that you will be able to save. When you practice this principle every chance you can, then one day you will be able to afford the newest, fanciest, or most popular item and still have financial stability in your life.

I myself struggle with wanting the latest in technology. I love reading about and exploring today's "gadgets." Sometimes I am able to say, "You know, I really do not need that." Sometimes I give in and allow myself to get something that is the latest, newest, or fanciest gadget. I do always try to determine whether I can really afford to spend the money at that time. Having the money and should I really spend the money are two different facts. It is challenging, but I try to think about both the short- and long-term consequences of spending money before making a purchase.

It is not easy, but I do know that if you always have to have more, more, more, that is an expensive habit to fuel.

DO NOT LOAN MONEY

Loaning money creates problems in all relationships. You want your money back, and they might not be able to repay it. When you loan money, no one wins.

I have advised people on several occasions that if you want to give someone money for a specific situation with no strings attached, then do that. Do not loan money and expect to get it back.

You may be willing to help someone, and they may sincerely want to pay it back. You should allow them to do so. It may be important to them. It is OK to loan it to them and let them pay it back. I just believe that it is best to loan it knowing in your heart that it might not come back. Then you will never be disappointed.

And do not guarantee other people's debts. In other words, do not cosign someone else's loans. They may mean well, just like if they borrow money from you, but their situation or decisions they make may mean they cannot repay their loan, and then you are on the hook for it. If you choose to do this, then realize that you may end up paying for that loan. If you are OK with that possibility, then fine.

INVEST IN YOURSELF

Education can never be taken away. The more you learn and increase your capabilities, the more value you will be able to deliver. When you deliver greater value, you have the right to receive greater value. If you can afford additional education or training in order to pursue a specific career you desire, then take the time and make the investment in yourself. Maybe you cannot afford the additional education at this time. That degree could be something for which you save. You can also make it a passion to learn in other ways. Seek out people who are successful and learn from them. Go to the library and read. It takes a commitment to learn and grow to take on new responsibilities in your professional life.

Each year my wife and I look for a way to experience personal development. Renee and I believe that personal growth should never stop. Besides the usual retreats and organized opportunities that exist, there are free speeches we attend at the community library. We have attended free summer concerts. There is a multitude of knowledge and information available today online that was non-existent just a few years ago.

The goal should be to make living these sound financial principles second nature. When you develop these habits and live them consistently, you get a result. Being committed to sound financial principles will impact your life, the lives of the people you work with, and certainly the lives of your family and people in your community.

Chapter 7

COMMITMENT TO HELPING INDIVIDUALS ACHIEVE THEIR POTENTIAL AND BE THEIR BEST

When someone believes in you, it goes a long way. Being believed in is a basic need.

I grew up in a family where I never heard a negative word about my pursuits. My parents never said I could not do something or that I was not able to achieve something. Not only did they never say anything negative about my potential; they were not neutral either. They were overtly positive about what I had the ability to do if I made a decision, paid the price, and applied myself. My parents saw my potential and then gave me the confidence and the support I needed to reach that potential. My parents allowed me to be the best that I could be. I would not be who I am today and be able to do what I do if they had not seen, believed in, encouraged, and supported my potential.

I was lucky. Not everyone grows up in that environment. I realize that.

Being believed in is a basic need.

Seeing potential is huge. It is the one thing that separates people being good from people being great. People cannot always see the potential in themselves. Having a leader or a coach see potential in someone helps that person be their best. When someone sees your potential, it helps you be your best; and when you see the potential in someone else and help them reach that potential, you help them be their best.

Many people do not understand the ability of being able to see and encourage someone's potential. The organizations that make this a part of what they are will achieve at a higher level because they are helping all of their people do the same.

When you believe that everyone has a purpose in their life, then you go about seeking that purpose and helping them realize that purpose. That is called making a difference in people's lives. And even though you are not seeking it, those people end up making a difference in your life.

When I first joined the board of directors of the National Speakers Association, the vice president, Rick Jakle, took me under his wing. At NSA, the vice president would become the president-elect and then the president. Rick asked me, a new board member, to be the meetings chairperson during the year that he would be president. Over the next three years, as he worked his way through the ranks, I worked with other volunteers to design and plan all of our meetings for the year that he was going to be president. At the same time, Rick kept calling me to discuss NSA business that was not part of my meetings responsibility. He kept me in the loop with agreements that needed to be dealt with, the renegotiation of the executive director's contract, and other such items. Rick appointed me as secretary of the organization the year he was president and made sure I was on the executive committee. Rick said to me, "One day you are going to be president of this organization, and I want you to be ready."

Rick saw potential in me. Rick believed in me. Rick wanted me to succeed. There was nothing in the energy and effort he was putting into my grooming and development that was for him. He was focused on me. He did not have to do that, but because of the leader that he was, he did.

Two years after Rick served as president I became the president of the National Speakers Association. That was an honor and a privilege that I will never forget, and it happened because someone saw potential in me and helped me achieve that potential.

A leader is always looking for potential. This is not a sometimes activity. You have to be selfless to see the potential in other people. You know it is not about you and your success. You genuinely want to see the people around you, in your family, in your community, or in your business, do better, be better, and see greater success and happiness.

This selfless approach is not common. Many people are focused only on their own success. These people may achieve some success, but they will achieve far more when they look at a person and sincerely strive to help them find and capture their potential.

It starts with actually listening to people when you talk with them. You hear them, you think about them, and you are concerned about them as people.

There is a joy that is derived from seeing others reach their potential. First, you see the potential in someone. Then, you move them toward it. What moves them toward it is, first, the relationship and, second, encouragement.

A leader is always looking for potential. This is not a sometimes activity.

Developing people is not training. Training is teaching someone how to do something over and over again.

Teaching someone how to use a new piece of software is training.

Developing people is about how people think and use their mind. Helping people evolve to a new way of thinking and believing is developing them and positioning them to grow and flourish.

My father was a veteran of World War II. He served in the Air Force. When he passed away, his casket was draped in the American flag. Prior to the casket being lowered into the ground, two members of the Air Force removed the flag and began to wrap it up. They folded it and folded it again. Then they began winding it into the shape of a triangle. They held the flag firmly in their grasp and carefully made each fold with precision until there was only the tail of the flag left to deal with.

Then one of the men cradled the triangle shaped flag in his arms as the other man dealt with the tail. You could see that he was holding the flag as he would hold a baby. The flag was secure in his arms, and no harm could come to it. The other airman gently folded the tail into the bundle, completing the triangle. The airman holding the folded flag then gently, with respect and concern, passed it to the other airman. The second airman then approached my mother and, with the utmost of respect for the flag and what it represented, tenderly presented the flag to her.

These two airmen exhibited respect, care, admiration, and concern for the flag, for what it represented, and for the man who fought to defend it. What if we looked at the people in our organization, our life, and our community the same way? It is that gentle, tender way of seeing people that is critical if we are to respect them, get to know them, and then be able to lead them to their potential. How we hold people in our eyes and in our minds is as important as how those airmen held that flag in their arms.

The first thing you are looking for in people is character, because you know if character is present, you can teach most any task and that person will be able to perform in new venues at a high level.

The leader has to be able to see the character of the individual and connect that to being able to reach a new potential. It is not just about physical skills. The leader believes that the character of the individual will allow them to go beyond anything they have done before.

Maybe it is as simple as believing that the individual would always be honest in any situation. Maybe it is just believing that the person will give it their best shot. Either way, it is a character decision, and it is the character of the individual that the leader is always on the lookout for.

Reaching potential is not an event. It takes time. Steps forward may be accompanied with steps backward, but the leader stays with the person regardless. The leader continues to support and encourage. Encouragement is at the core of helping someone reach their potential. Constant encouragement is critical.

How you see and value people will drive this. If you see people as "less than," you probably will not look for that potential. You also probably will not spend time getting to know people and discovering what they really could be. Gratitude is at the heart of valuing people, and this is how you see their potential.

When you live a life of gratitude, you are not just thankful for the gifts that come your way. You are not just grateful for your portion and your possessions. You are grateful for everything. You are grateful for the sun rising in the morning and the rain watering the plants, and you certainly are grateful for people. In truth, people who live a life of sincere gratitude are thankful not only for the people they know but also for the people they do not know. They are grateful for the people they have just met. And they are grateful for people even if they look different, act differently, and think differently than they do. Gratitude is all about being thankful for the people around you and expressing that feeling through the deeds you perform on their behalf. Finding and leading someone to their potential may be the best deed you can perform.

Discrimination will eliminate the ability to see the potential in someone. Viewing people differently because of race, religion, gender, physical attributes, or personal style choices means you will always miss out on seeing their potential. When leaders do this, they essentially rob the people they lead of a more promising future, and they rob their organization of talent, ideas, and a better looking bottom line.

There can be no place for prejudice, bias, or racism in an organization or in the mind and heart of an individual. Prejudice is an unfair feeling or dislike because of race, sex, religion, or other descriptive factor. Bias is when you feel that some people are better than others or that their ideas are better. Racism manifests itself in the poor treatment of people based strictly on race. All three of these will blind you and keep you from seeing the potential of the people you lead or the people in your life.

Discrimination eliminates the ability to see the potential in someone.

A few years ago, I had a dinner with the chief operating officer (COO) of a company that was a client of mine. The dinner was on the evening of the first day of a two-day conference. The first day, during the meeting, I listened as the COO addressed 500 middle managers and told his people that the company could not have had the great year they had without them.

That night at dinner, the COO looked at me and said, "Tomorrow when you speak, no one in the room has a college degree. Keep it simple. If you just give them three or four good points, you will do great."

I was appalled. This COO had just made a determination of his people's potential based on their education. He unknowingly showed his prejudice against his middle managers because they did not have a college degree. He did not know why they did not have a degree, and he did not know what their capabilities really were. He placed a limit on his people and tried to transfer it to me.

What he should have done at dinner was to lean across the table and say, "Sam, I have the best managers on the planet. I want you to give your very best to them. Don't you dare hold back. You give my people everything you have!"

This was a good guy. He didn't mean to stereotype. But with that mind-set, he will not lead people to be their best. No one will lead people to be their best if prejudice, racism, and bias are in the way.

Something changes in a person when they know that someone else believes in them. When you know that someone believes in you, you start to believe in yourself at a higher level. Once this happens, people develop confidence. Then all of a sudden they start to take on challenges on their own. When someone invests in you, you do not want to let them down. When someone sees your potential and helps you achieve that potential, you value them even more, and loyalty is created between you.

When a company hires from outside the organization, hope and potential may be diminished. Sometimes you have to hire outside of the organization. Sometimes you do not. When you do have to and you have not looked for the ability or potential inside and developed it, that is the problem. If the leaders are doing what they are supposed to be doing, then they will always be developing people both for the individual's growth and for the future potential needs that the organization is going to have.

When you see potential in people and help them to be successful in reaching that potential, then you are able to promote from within and, in so doing, give everyone greater hope that their future is brighter and that there are possibilities for personal growth and development for them in that organization. You are providing them with a reason to stay and build toward the future.

Developing people is the supreme responsibility of leadership. Discovering potential is encouragement at the highest level. Yes, it takes effort. People want leadership to be easy, but it does not work that way. Leadership requires something of the leader. Leadership in not just a bigger check, a bigger office, and a place to park your car. Leadership is a responsibility. The commitment to discover the potential of the people you lead is at the top of the list of your responsibilities.

It is critical to the ultimate performance of an organization that the leadership has the ability to see the potential in people. This connects directly to the bottom line. Every time you help someone reach their potential you have created an individual that will deliver more value to the organization. What happens in an organization when every-one delivers more value this year than last?

A commitment to helping individuals achieve their potential and be their best is a commitment to the people in your life and your organization. That commitment is felt and returned. When you develop your people, they can reach that potential no matter what, and they will be willing to help you achieve your goals, no matter what.

Chapter 8

COMMITMENT TO A SAFE PLACE TO WORK

I was a partner in a window and door manufacturing business. Productivity was a big thing for me. I wanted the sales team to be productive, I wanted the office staff to be productive, and I certainly wanted our manufacturing plant to have the highest productivity possible.

Quite frankly, our window production was weak. We did not get the orders completed very quickly, and the quality was not consistent. The more we, the leadership, pushed, the worse it got. The more we complained, the more nothing changed.

We were losing money fast and were close to going out of business when we changed the way we thought about things. We decided to let the people in the plant "take over." We empowered them to design how the equipment would be laid out, how the orders would be processed, what goals would be set, and how they would go about achieving those goals. We got off their backs and started supporting them.

Ultimately, we started seeing the people not as the problem but as the keys to the solutions. And solve the situation they did. Less than two months after we created a place where they could safely say what they wanted and make the changes they needed and gave them the assurance that if they spoke, we listened to them and heard them, things changed. We went from having slow turnaround times and inconsistent quality to having incredibly fast production times and fantastic quality. Our customers immediately noticed the difference. And that difference showed up in the bottom line as profits instead of losses.

While I am embarrassed to admit it, looking back I now realize that I saw the people who worked there as an expense. They were "costing" us money. The reality is that they were an asset, and they were the ones who could make things better. I was lucky that we started seeing and treating the people differently.

Yes, productivity and profits are important, but it is a mistake to focus on those things first. When you focus first on people and creating a safe place for them to work, then they focus on productivity and creating profits. They are thankful for the safe environment that you have created. The people know that their productivity will benefit everyone, including themselves.

Today, I fully understand what it means to see people as different, with prejudice. I know that we are really all the same. We may have different jobs and different responsibilities, but we are all people who just want an opportunity to make a difference, make a living, and take care of our families. We need a safe environment in which to do that.

I know that workplace safety is important. When I talk about a commitment to a safe place to work, I am not talking about physical safety. At my company, we also consult and work with companies who want their organizational culture to reinforce the importance of safety because of the inherent risks that exist in their industry, whether it be mining or electrical transmission. Of course that is important. However, many organizations focus on the physical safety of their employees but overlook their emotional and spiritual safety.

Think about where you work. Is it safe to bring a new idea to leadership? Is it safe to ask when you do not understand something? Is it safe to challenge the leader's idea? At what point do you yield to authority? Is it safe to question the status quo? It is safe emotionally?

If the answer to any of these questions is "no," then I would say that it is not the safe place that every place of business should be.

Many organizations focus on the physical safety of their employees but overlook their emotional and spiritual safety.

When you commit to a safe place to work, there is a protection of, a caring for, a nurturing of people. There is freedom in a safe place. There is freedom of thought, innovation, and creativity. In a safe workplace, you can discover your very best because you can be who you really are. When you are your true, authentic self, you are always going to operate at your very best.

Spiritual growth, the ability to seek and understand who you are, takes place in a safe place. People are not judging you based on skin color, socioeconomic status, and other ways that someone might judge you. You are not hindered. This frees you up. You can apply and utilize your God-given gifts, and in that environment, you grow to be your best.

When everyone in an organization can grow to be their best, then the organization grows to be its best. When you create a safe place, and creativity and innovation are allowed to roam free, you create an organization that always finds better procedures and creates better products and services and one that transforms into the absolute leader in their industry.

When you have a safe place, you do not have to worry about politics. You do not have to worry about how you are going to be treated. Distractions are eliminated. You can just focus on your job and getting the results you are working toward.

You do not mandate creativity, teamwork, customer service, and accountability. You create a safe place and allow those elements to flourish naturally and to their very highest potential. And people always want to go to a safe place. We all enjoy the feeling of safety. When the people look forward to going to work and being safe, you have created a powerful competitive advantage.

When a leader values people, trusts people, builds relationships, communicates in the Terms of Change™ (as mentioned in chapter 4), and is accountable, they create an emotionally safe place. Even though a company may be facing all kinds of change both internally and externally, knowing that you work in a safe place offers an inner peace that allows you to focus on what you need to focus on. This consistent, steady focus positions you and your organization to excel.

Ultimately, it is the values that make an environment safe. Values are always about people. When the values are well thought out, clear, and adhered to, a safe place emerges. Living the values, not just having them on a piece of paper, is essential. It comes down to leadership. Leadership determines if it is a safe place or not by how they live the values. What the leader models, teaches, and protects determines if the environment is actually a safe place.

The people are always going to do what the leader does. It is a simple game of follow the leader. We used to play it all the time when we were kids. We know how it works. Everyone always looks to the leader. The leader creates the safe place.

The values make an environment safe.

This, like all of the ten commitments in this book, is a way of thinking. Leaders are looking out for the people they lead. They care about people. They would never want the workplace to be any less safe than someone's home.

Some leaders will say, "But this isn't the home. This is the workplace." My response would be, "Do you want the best out of people or do you want half or three-quarters of what they can do?"

Phrases such as "This is business" and "This is a place of business" have no business showing up. An organization is made up of people who deserve a safe place to get their work done.

Leaders also work hard to establish relationships. They establish the relationship from the very beginning. The relationship is formed through the physical, through face-to-face interactions. When you develop a strong, positive relationship with people, you create a connection where people feel safe with you. All great relationships have trust at their core because when people trust you, they feel safe.

It is the leader's responsibility to create and protect the organizational culture. Creating an organizational culture takes effort and commitment. The leader who creates an organizational culture where safety is a priority does so through five specific steps.

DESIGN IT

The culture is designed through the values. If the values are not discovered and clearly defined, then you get a culture by default. When the values are specific and clear, they say, "This is how we do it here." It is through the values that people know if they can talk to someone when they are having a problem at home or if it is safe to bring new ideas. A leader honors new ideas no matter the source. They realize that they thrive on new ideas. This ultimately simplifies change. Change is what will automatically flow from the point in time that you make a decision to improve some aspect of your life or your business.

MODEL IT

When the culture flows from the leader, it naturally flows to all of the people. When the leader models safety through transparency and sharing from their personal life, then the people feel safe sharing the events in their life that they need help with also. When the leader lives the values to a level of non-negotiable and they don't make or accept any exceptions for living the value, then the people will live the value consistently too. When the leader values people and their actions fully support this, then the people will value those around them. The leader must align their actions with their words first before they can expect their people to act that way.

Teach It

What gets taught gets tested. Every day in an organization, as in a life, your values are going to get tested. Every decision that everyone makes is going to be a test of the values. You must continually teach the values so that the people always know what they are. Then, when a customer comes up that is irate, your people will know what to do based on the values.

The people know that the leadership has their back when they make decisions based on the values because the leaders are not asking the people to do anything that they are not doing themselves. And in the conversations they have with their people, leaders always connect every decision they make to the values. This is instruction through real-life situations.

Protect It

It is non-negotiable. Never make an exception on creating and maintaining an emotionally safe place to work. Never make an exception on a value either. Through their values, a leader defines and spells out specifically how they are going to treat each other within the company. That creates an environment of safety.

In my book *Non-Negotiable*, I share the story of Pat Hickman, CEO of Happy State Bank, and how Pat and his team have built an amazingly successful organization through their values. Their values are well thought out, very clear, and taught to everyone. Most importantly, they protect those values by never allowing anyone in the organization not to live all of their values. It is the responsibility of the people at Happy State Bank to know and fully live those values within the organization—no exceptions. No exceptions on any of the values, and no exceptions for any of the employees of the bank, not even the CEO.

When the values of an organization or individual are non-negotiable, then you are protecting them and the culture they create. It is that simple and that powerful. I once had a potential client say, "Isn't that a little idealistic?" My answer was, "No!" But in that moment I knew that they would never hire me to help solve their accountability problems. The leadership was not willing to commit to their stated values. When that happens, no one else in the organization will commit either.

Ultimately, you protect your culture when you take a stand and say, "This is how we do it here. It is not negotiable for any reason."

CELEBRATE IT

When you don't feel encouraged, you are not in the presence of a true leader. A leader is always thankful for the people that work for them. Sincere gratitude always makes people feel valued. Heavy on the sincere! And that creates a safe place.

Make the time to thank people individually and to create the time and place to celebrate personal and organizational successes as a team. The people around you need to know you appreciate and value them. This not only reinforces how you feel about them and their importance to the organization and its goals and mission, but it also ensures that the organizational culture you have created is a safe place.

At Happy State Bank, it was safe for an employee to go to the CEO and tell him that her husband had cancer. There are some organizations where that would never happen for fear of losing one's job. At Happy State Bank, she felt safe enough to share intimate details about her personal life.

At home you feel safe. You lay around, you kick off your shoes, and you relax. Because Pat, the CEO of the bank, is the same at work as he is at home, he creates a safe place everywhere he goes. Pat immediately set up for this employee to work from home. He installed a computer and the necessary secure network connect to make it happen.

This happened because Happy State Bank's values are about people. This happened because those values apply across the board, to everyone. This happened because the leader knows only one way to treat people. Because their environment is safe, the employees at Happy State Bank figure out how to solve problems—problems at work as well as personal problems. This is an incredibly safe environment. And this is an incredibly loyal, inspired, engaged group of employees—all because of the safe environment.

Leaders are always doing everything with the people in mind. They are always all about the people. The values are all about the people. Their focus is all about the people. Their focus is relationships. They know that if their people are happy, the business is going to kick butt. People who truly value people and people who truly lead are going to design their culture accordingly. They will always be committed to a safe place to work.

Chapter 9

COMMITMENT TO YOUR WORD IS YOUR BOND

A bond is a vow, a promise, something that holds things together. A bond is something that is solid and strong, something that withstands. Nothing is going to break it.

When your word is your bond, you are saying, "If I said it, I meant it!" Your word is your bond, and absolutely nothing will break it. What happens when your word is your bond is that you are not just "bonding" to what you said you would do, but you are also creating a bond between you and another person. This bond is a commitment to a relationship, and it is the relationship that is at stake.

The commitment of your word is your bond speaks to the character of a person. People whose word is their bond believe that it is the right thing to do to deliver on what you committed to. There is no middle ground here. If you keep your word only some of the time, it is the same as if your word is never your bond. This is a very black-and-white issue. Your word is your bond, or it is not. You are a liar, or you are not.

This all goes toward credibility. There are certain people whom we never believe anything that comes out of their mouth. They have lost credibility because their word is not their bond. Their word does not mean anything at all.

Without credibility you cannot be believed. If you cannot be believed, then no one can or will follow you. If no one is willing to follow you, you cannot be a leader.

When you have credibility, people trust you and believe everything you say. As long as you never give people a reason to question your credibility, you will create a powerful position. The power of people believing you, standing behind you, supporting you in your mission, and spreading a kind and positive word about you is immeasurable!

But you have to be worthy to be believed. What does it mean to be "worthy" to be believed? It means that you have merit and strength of character. It means that your actions over time, as they connect to what you said you will do, must align, be just, and be consistent. When you are worthy to be believed, you create credibility.

A leader's power depends on their credibility.

When your word is your bond, you position yourself to have influence. Influence means that people are listening to you. They hear you. They want to respond to what you say and adjust their actions because they trust you. When you have influence, people will perform at a higher level than they thought possible. With influence you have the ability to encourage people, guide people, and shape the decisions that people make. Influence is powerful. Positive influence harnesses that power to achieve good and meaningful results.

When you have influence over someone's life, you are creating a subtle flow of thought and care that has the ability to move that person to action. A leader with influence can impact the direction someone takes, help someone be their best, and improve the trajectory of events in that individual's life.

Influence is often underappreciated. This powerful connection can help people reach their potential. When your influence is powered by love and caring, you will speak into the lives of people in a way that will not only grow them as people but will grow a bond between you that can last a lifetime. Your impact on them through your influence will make a difference in them and in your relationship with them.

Influence is a major part of a leader's legacy toolkit. It is through influence that you create a lasting legacy of positive results. Your influence as a leader positions you to impact your organization, your community, your family, and beyond. That influence, when shaped in a positive manner, can be transformative.

Making your word your bond also connects to authority. Authority is the power to lead. There is both positional authority and relational authority. In many cases, positional authority comes with a job title. The CEO of a company has positional authority. The president of the United States has positional authority. This authority is real and allows you to accomplish things.

However, your real authority is derived from the opinion, respect, and esteem that is created in the minds of the people around you. This authority flows from the relationships you build. Authority is earned though those relationship over time and as a result of your actions. Relational authority is incredibly powerful.

Positional authority is simply created by title or position and may be seen as forced on people. Because of the character of the leader, people may not really want to follow the person with positional authority.

The relational authority that you earn through your actions and how people see and connect to you is natural and the most powerful. This authority gives you the ability to accomplish significant goals and tasks. In this situation, people are actively choosing to listen to you and follow you. Your authority has not been forced on them. Your authority is born through the depth of your relationships with people.

> **Your real authority is derived from the opinion, respect, and esteem that is created in the minds of the people around you.**

A leader recognizes this power, values it, and never abuses it. This power, derived from your relationships, gives you the ability to lead people in a direction that will yield a result. In an organization, that result should be tied to your goal and mission.

There are people who could have influence and not have any authority. You can have positional authority and not have credibility or influence. Authority, credibility, and influence are totally separate. When you have both positional authority and relational authority combined with credibility and influence, you will move mountains, change the course of direction of people's lives, and have a significant impact in your community.

Credibility, authority, and influence combine to create a powerful combination. If you lack credibility, authority, and influence, it becomes difficult, if not impossible, to accomplish anything meaningful in your personal and professional life. You lack the ability to attract people to your cause, to motivate them, and to create an impact that requires a body of people greater than just you.

You have to have all three attributes in order to be the consummate leader. With all three qualities you will effectively lead a business, community, or family. If one of those attributes is missing, you will always come up short, never achieving the impact that you could potentially create.

> **When you have both positional authority and relational authority combined with credibility and influence, you will move mountains**

When you have credibility, authority, and influence, you attract others to your cause and mission. You have the ability to rally them to move forward to accomplish goals and deliver on a mission. You are positioned to shape their lives positively, the lives of their families, and the lives of the people they touch. Credibility, authority, and influence extend your reach vastly beyond what it normally would be because you can say anything and people are going to stand by you.

To commit to your word is your bond, you have to believe that such a commitment is important. It is that simple. If you believe it, you will live it. If you do not believe it, you will not. If something is important, you do it. If it is not important, you do not.

You may want to argue this point, but it is irrefutable. Why would anyone who says they believe something not live it? It does not work that way. If you really believe something, then it has to consistently show up in your actions. I know that there can be challenging times. There can be times when it is hard to live all of your values. However, when you believe something, you do not look for a way out of that belief or value; you get creative and find a way to live it!

I have the honor of managing my mother's finances. As part of that responsibility, I needed to sell a commercial building that she owned. My real estate agent was approached by a buyer, and we began negotiating the sale of the building. Ultimately, we agreed on an "as is" price for the building and a quick closing.

Then, the buyer wanted to have his contractor inspect the building. They decided that an air conditioning unit on the roof was not working and that they were going to deduct 50 thousand dollars at closing or they would not buy the building. I reminded them that the original offer was "as is." I also said, "Fine. If you are not going to live up to your end of the bargain, then the sale is off. I accept your offer not to buy the building." Immediately, they said that we had had an agreement and that they would sue me.

Once they said they would not buy the property unless I lowered the price, the door opened for me to end the agreement morally and legally. I consulted my attorney, and he confirmed my understanding of the situation.

We later found out that they had a reputation of offering a good price to buy a property "as is," but then, if the price was not lowered at closing due to some undisclosed issue they seemed to discover, they would threaten to sue.

The deal was off. I was ready to find a new buyer. Their problem was that they still wanted to buy the building. Because the original agreement had been voided and we were now starting a new negotiation, I told my agent that I would not sell it at the same price; the price had gone up. I told my agent that I was adding on a "nuisance" fee, as the buyer's nonsense was adding extra work for my agent, and I had incurred additional legal fees because of the buyer's lack of commitment.

I informed my agent of the new, slightly higher price I wanted him to present to the buyer, along with the instruction that I would not negotiate. I instructed him to tell the buyer specifically that if they tried to negotiate, I would not sell the building to them at any price. I was done with their games. My agent said, "Wow. That is a great negotiating strategy."

I told him, "It is not a negotiating strategy. My word is my bond. I expect the people with whom I do business to act in the same manner. If they cannot, I will not to do business with them. This is how I choose to operate."

In that moment, my agent knew that if I said it, I meant it. He knew that this was not a negotiation technique or a bluff to get a higher price. I said it, and I meant it, period.

He knew that he could not come back to me with a negotiated price and expect me to accept it. He was good with my position.

The credibility that I had with my real estate agent positioned him in the best and strongest possible position to go back to the purchaser and deal straight with him. In the end, we sold the building at the higher price and closed quickly.

By living this way, I always know my position; it is exactly what I said it would be. I never have to reconsider my commitment. All I have to do is execute and move forward. It is simple. It is clean. It works! On top of all that, my relationship with my real estate agent was stronger because he saw me living my word is my bond.

When you commit to your word is your bond, people always know where you stand and where they stand with you. Ultimately, they know you always stand with them, they know you support them, and they know you are not going to disappear when they need to count on you most.

It is important to know what you believe and what you value. Do not say it if it is not what you believe and what you value. People might say something because it is catchy or they think that someone wants to hear it, but it is not what they truly believe. We can tell that it is not what they truly believe because their actions do not line up with their words.

Do not say it if you are not going to do it. As a supervisor, do not tell an employee you are going to review them in six months and then not do it. There is no excuse not to do what you say you are going to do.

If you say it, others should be able to take it to the bank. It should happen. Your character is defined in the minds of others when what you say always happens.

There are specific characteristics of an accountable leader that make their word their bond. Those characteristics are mercy, kindness, humility, patience, and forgiveness. When a leader is living these characteristics, then they will commit to their word.

These are qualities that can be learned. These attributes create excellence. Excellence is being of great value or use. People who live their lives by these qualities and commit to their word is their bond create value and worth in everything they do and in every relationship they build. Leaders bring excellence every single time they walk into the room.

The values are the leader's bond. The values are laid out in black and white, and a leader is totally committed to them. Leaders are committed to their personal values, and they are just as committed to the organizational values. It is their word. It is solid. It is impenetrable, unbreakable. You can count on it. When a leader's word is their bond, it creates an atmosphere of trust. When you have trust, then you create an environment filled with peacefulness. I know I can trust you, and I do not have to continuously watch my back for what you might do.

In a place of peace, a state of tranquility, people are free to be their best, operate at their best level, and achieve their best results. When a leader brings this to an organization, the people and the organization thrive. When a leader brings this to their family, their family thrives.

When you commit to your word is your bond, it is as if you are eight feet tall in a room of people who are only five feet tall; you stand out. Your character, veracity, and moral being stand out. They attract others to you and position you to move forward successfully while setting a positive example that the people around you will want to emulate.

Ultimately, by committing to your word is your bond, the place of peace that you have created for everyone around you will have you placed right in the center, enjoying that same peace in your life.

Chapter 10

COMMITMENT TO A GOOD REPUTATION

What are you known for? Are you known for showing up on time? Or are you known for always being late? Are you known for being kind? Are you known for being a critical thinker? Maybe you are known for being smart, or trustworthy. Or maybe you are known for being deceitful or manipulative. However you are known and thought of by others constitutes your reputation. Good or bad, you create your reputation over time through your actions. Your reputation is how others see your character.

One quality that defines a person that has a good reputation is humility. Living with humility does not mean that you are not a gregarious, passionate, and confident businessperson. Humility means that you are not motivated by selfish ambition. It means that you are confident but not conceited. You do not think more highly of yourself than you ought, and you focus on and look for the good in everyone around you. Remember gratitude?

While it is certainly OK to look out for your own interests, when you live with humility you are certain to look out for the interests of others. You do this because you value them. You want them to get ahead. These all lead to humility, which is the primary characteristic that leads to a good reputation.

Humility is the primary characteristic that leads to a good reputation.

You cannot lead without a good reputation. People will not follow you wholeheartedly if you do not have a good reputation. They may follow you out of obligation. They may follow you because they need their paycheck. But they will never stand up for you, and they will leave at the first opportunity. They will leave for a nickel more pay because they are not truly following you; they are just doing the minimal amount required in order to collect their check.

When someone believes in your good reputation, they want to be a part of that, and they will follow you to the ends of the earth. They will protect your good reputation. They will fight for it. They will produce at a level never imagined or otherwise achieved.

Your good reputation becomes an umbrella for the people who associate with you. People are attracted to your reputation, and they benefit personally from having a relationship with you. Your good reputation helps them build their good reputation.

When I was in the window and door manufacturing business, I was partners with my father-in-law and brother-in-law. We experienced a lot in that business, both positive and, at times, challenging events. I learned a lot in that business about what a reputation really was and the power of a good reputation.

My father-in-law, Mendel, was an amazing example to me of how to build relationships and trust with people. We went to Boston once to make a presentation to a potentially large account. If successful, the new client would add two million dollars in business annually. I made the presentation and showed the two gentlemen sitting across from us why our product, service, and customer support would position them to grow their business faster and more profitably.

After a back-and-forth conversation, the owner of the company said, "Let's make this happen. Send me the paperwork to sign, and we can get started." With that, my father-in-law stood up, reached his hand across the table, and said, "My word is my bond."

Now Mendel had been around the industry for some time. He had a reputation built on many years of paying his bills on time, delivering a product as promised, and doing whatever he said he would do when he said he would do it. He had worked with others in our industry at meetings and even served as the president of our national trade association.

Tony, our prospective client, stood up and shook Mendel's hand. He then shook my hand, and my father-in-law and I both shook the hand of the other gentleman sitting at the table. We had just finalized a 2 million dollar annual deal with a handshake! This handshake deal was based on a reputation that had been forged by someone who lived his values over a long period of time. My father-in-law's reputation actually became a competitive advantage for us as an organization, not only with this client, but with many other clients as well.

My father-in-law's good reputation spread to cover me as well. People in our industry very quickly saw me in the same light as they had seen him. I had gained a good reputation within our industry simply through association. This inspired me to want to act only in a way that would honor and protect that reputation. I became committed to a good reputation. I leveraged that good reputation to an over 430 percent organizational growth over the years I was part of the ownership team of the company.

Sometimes, when people meet face to face for the first time, someone will say, "Your reputation precedes you." When this is true and believed, it creates a positive first impression and positions you for success in that relationship. It is a powerful place to be.

If, as Heraclitus said, "Character is destiny," then having good character will lead to a good destiny. Our future is created in part as we create our character. Our reputation is defined, connected to, and seen through our character.

A commitment to a good reputation starts with discovering what you value and building a solid foundation.

Your reputation starts with your values, but it grows through the stories that are told about how you live those values. Your reputation is built through others. How you live your values impacts other people. You impact the lives of everyone with whom you come in contact through your values. Those contact points with people and the way you treat them and act toward them create impressions. People turn those impressions into a belief of what your character is and how they define your reputation. Ultimately, you create your reputation in the minds of the people in your life, both personally and professionally.

The seeds of a good reputation are planted in the values you choose and how you go about living those values. Based on these values and the way in which you live your values, the people around you make judgments regarding your character. The people with whom you interact spread these judgments to others through comments regarding their interactions with you, creating and furthering your reputation.

Values alone will not create a good reputation. You must be consistent in how you live those values for your reputation to be a good one. When you are steady in your values, people see you as reliable and dependable. When it comes to character—and a character that is based on strong values—consistent, committed, and steady are the attributes that yield the best results.

Accountability plays a big role in building a good reputation. If accountability is keeping your commitments to people, then it matters how you treat other people.

> **The seeds of a good reputation are planted in the values you choose and how you go about living those values.**

Ultimately, all values are about people. It will always come back to "How are you treating people?" Valuing people is at the very core of a commitment to a good reputation. People want to be valued. People know when you value them, and they certainly know when you do not.

When you value people, you treat them with respect and honor; and when you treat them with respect and honor, then they see you in a very positive light. When you value people, there is a reciprocal reaction that produces loyalty, honor, trust, and credibility. And it produces a good reputation. When you are truly grateful for people, you can value them, their abilities, and ultimately their humanness.

Bad reputations can be formed rather quickly. Good reputations can be destroyed rather quickly. But a good reputation is created over time. A monetary investment takes time to grow and pay dividends. So does a good reputation. It takes a commitment.

Think about someone you know who always does the right thing. The right thing is usually the hard thing. It is the tough decisions that lead to a good reputation. Anyone can do the right thing when it is easy, but when there is a cost to you, when you have to sacrifice and you still do the right thing, people see that. If you are living your values in those tough moments and making decisions that truly align with great values, then your character grows. Your good reputation will grow also. A good reputation comes at a cost. There is an investment on our part that creates a good reputation. A commitment to a good reputation is a commitment to always doing what is right.

Sometimes you are going to have to fight for something, even if it is not the popular decision. When you fight for the truth, it builds your good reputation. When you fight to do what is right, that builds your good reputation. You will run into many people who want to take the quick and easy way out. They are willing to sacrifice the truth, pass up on doing what is right, just to move on.

Fighting for something you believe in adds to your reputation in two ways. First, you become known for doing what is right, even if it is not popular or takes extra effort. Second, your character grows, in that people know you will not back down when you believe in something. They know you will support your values and that you do not take the easy way. These two recognitions combined build a character that attracts others to you and your causes.

When you say, "We are going to do what is right, no matter what," there may be a cost. You may miss out on something you want to do because of something you said you would do. You may have to suppress your desires in order to fulfill someone else's. You may have to fire someone and then work extra yourself in order to stay caught up. But you do what is right, not what is easy.

There is something about taking the high road that, while difficult at times, will always take you to your desired destination.

I mentioned commitment, consistency, and being steady. It is through these attributes that you not only create your good reputation but protect it. Being committed to your values no matter what, you stay steady. The people who hold you in high regard, who believe in your good reputation, and who follow you will also step up and protect that reputation. They will speak highly of you and oppose those individuals who might try to say something that is not true about you. They will help defend your good reputation.

When you are committed to a good reputation, people become committed to you. Your good reputation will extend beyond your personal reach as the reputation forged in the minds of others is shared with broader circles, including people with whom you may never interact. And when you do come in contact with one of those individuals, they just might say, "Your good reputation precedes you."

THE WORLD IS NOW YOUR RESPONSIBILITY ALSO

Renee and I attended the wedding of our friend's daughter recently. The bride had gone to school with our daughter, Allison. Before the wedding started, I texted Allison, who is a first-year medical resident, to let her know whose wedding we were at, and Allison responded, "Since when are my friends old enough to be getting married?" I laughed. She then added, "Along those lines, I ask myself regularly, how the heck am I a doctor?" I laughed again.

I am very proud of Allison and the difference she works to make in the lives of other people. As I do with all of my children, I believe in Allison and her mission. I replied to her, "The world is now your responsibility also."

For those of you reading this book, at this very moment the world is your responsibility also. It is time for all of us to stand up and accept the Ten Commitments of Accountability, to live accountable lives, and to set the expectation of accountability for the people around us. It is time for No Matter What to become an integral part of what we believe and how we act and the mantra we share and teach to our family, friends, and associates.

With a No Matter What mind-set, you can change the world and make it better

One person can change the world. You may make a big difference. You may only change a small part, but you can change the world and make it better. When enough people work to change a small part, it adds up, and those changes lead to larger changes. It really does start with you, just as I believe it starts with me. Do not worry about how big or small the change is. Take the first step.

Accountability is keeping your commitments to people, and a commitment is No Matter What. Accountability is not a way of doing; it is a way of thinking. Commitment is a way of thinking. This all enables you to be the leader you can be, by accepting the responsibility that comes with leadership. That responsibility is for the people you lead. Remember, accountability is the highest form of leadership.

Accountability is all about valuing and honoring people. That honor starts with commitments—me keeping mine and you keeping yours.

The 10 Commitments of Accountability

1. Commitment to the truth
2. Commitment to what you value
3. Commitment to "It's all of us"
4. Commitment to stand with you when all hell breaks loose
5. Commitment to the faults and failures as well as the opportunities and successes
6. Commitment to sound financial principles
7. Commitment to helping individuals achieve their potential and be their best
8. Commitment to a safe place to work
9. Commitment to your word is your bond
10. Commitment to a good reputation

When the Accountable Leader keeps these commitments, not only do they create a place where people want to be, but they develop an army of future accountable leaders. People by nature will act the way the leader acts.

With whom do you want to surround yourself—people who keep their commitments or people who do not?

Sometimes you do not have a choice. You may not have a choice whom you work with or what is allowed in your organization. Leaders have a choice. They can allow individuals in an organization to fail to keep their commitments. Or they can choose to say, "We keep our commitments here. I keep mine, and you keep yours or you will need to find another place to work."

If you are going to commit:

1. **You have to believe it is important.**
2. **You have to believe it is the right thing to do.**
3. **You have to believe it is what you are supposed to do.**

People who keep their commitments do so because it is important to them. If it is important to us, we do it.

I never said this is going to be easy. Commitment really only shows up when it is not easy. Commitment to the truth is going to get hard. Commitment to sound financial principles is going to get difficult when you need to put food on the table. It is important to know that.

Commitments are not easy, but they produce. With commitment, you create relationships, trust, collaboration, teamwork, and innovation. Commitments are going to get hard, but you will never experience the joy that comes on the back end if you give up in the middle.

It will always come down to this: Are you looking for a way in or are you looking for a way out?

Join me in my commitment to No Matter What. Discover our free newsletter and the many resources we have at www.SamSilverstein.com. Get your friends, family, and coworkers on board, living the mantra of No Matter What. Accept no less in your life, in your organization, and in your community.

When you believe that living these ten commitments will make a difference in your life, you will live them. When you believe they will make a difference in the lives of the people around you, you will share them with those people.

This is not just something you do this month and then move on to another great idea next month. When No Matter What becomes who you are, then you live it daily.

Let's create a world where people keep their commitments.

Let's create a world where people want to be accountable.

Let's create a world of which we are sincerely proud to be a part.

Let's start today!

ABOUT THE AUTHOR

SAM SILVERSTEIN is founder and CEO of Sam Silverstein, Incorporated, an accountability think tank dedicated to helping companies create an organizational culture that prioritizes and inspires accountability. By helping organizations develop what they believe in, clarify their mission, and understand what is in their control, Sam works to make this a more accountable world. He is the author of several books, including *No More Excuses*, *Non-Negotiable*, *No Matter What*, *The Success Model*, and *The Lost Commandments*. He speaks internationally, having worked with teams of companies, government agencies, communities, and organizations both big and small, including Kraft Foods, Pfizer, the United States Air Force, and United Way. Sam is the past president of the National Speakers Association.